Richard C[...]
Plays [...]

Can't Stand Up for Falling Down, Pond Life, The Mortal Ash, All of You Mine

Can't Stand Up for Falling Down: 'As a record of one man's heartless destructiveness, Cameron's play is itself cumulatively and salutarily devastating ... Building up a picture from many partial perspectives, the monologues are beautifully arranged.' *Independent*

Pond Life: 'the unpatronisingly sensitive vignette of adolescence explores more angles than angling in these youngsters' lives. Cameron is plainly a man to watch.' *Mail on Sunday*
'Dialogue is sharp and authentic. Cameron has already established his alert ear for young people's talk, and he reveals a comparable skill for the guarded, and unguarded, disputes between them and their parents.' *The Times*

The Mortal Ash: 'Over the past few years, Cameron has emerged as the shrewd chronicler of a small-town, post industrial England whose experience is quite distinct from that of city dwellers. The Mortal Ash is his best play yet.' *Guardian*

All of You Mine: ' ... a fine work, buttressed by rich, jagged dialogue ringing authentic to my northern ear.' *Punch*
' ... there is a remorseless, Ibsen-like vigour about the way he uncovers lies, motives and bad faith.' *Sunday Times*

Richard Cameron was born in Doncaster, South Yorkshire. He taught for many years, was Director of Scunthorpe Youth Theatre from 1979 to 1988 and Head of Drama at the Thomas Sumpter School in Scunthorpe until 1991, then gave up teaching in order to write full-time. His plays include *Haunted Flowers*, now retitled *Handle with Care*, (National Student Drama Festival and Edinburgh Fringe Festival, 1985) which won the 1985 Sunday Times Playwriting Award; *Strugglers* (Battersea Arts Centre, 1988), which won the 1988 Sunday Times Playwriting Award; the *Moon's the Madonna* (NSDF, Edinburgh Fringe Festival and Battersea Arts Centre, 1989), which was shortlisted for the Independent Theatre Award and won the 1989 Company Award at the NSDF and *Can't Stand Up for Falling Down* (Edinburgh Fringe Festival and Hampstead Theatre, London) for which he won the Sunday Times Playwriting Award for a record third time in 1990, as well as a Scotsman Fringe First and the 1990 Independent Theatre Award. *Pond Life* (Bush Theatre, London, 1992), *Not Fade Away* (Bush Theatre, 1993). *The Mortal Ash* (Bush Theatre), *Almost Grown* (Royal National Theatre, London), and *Seven* (Birmingham Rep.) all performed in 1994. *With Every Beat* (West Yorkshire Playhouse, 1995) and *In Bed With Billy Cotton* (Belgrade Theatre, Conventry) and *All of You Mine* (Bush Theatre) in 1996. His first television play *Stone Scissors Paper* won the inaugural BBC Television Dennis Potter Play of the Year Award in 1995.

RICHARD CAMERON

Plays: 1

Can't Stand Up for Falling Down
Pond Life
The Mortal Ash
All of You Mine

introduced by the author

Methuen Drama

METHUEN CONTEMPORARY DRAMATISTS

This collection first published in Great Britain in 1998
by Methuen Drama
Random House, 20 Vauxhall Bridge Road, London SW1 2SA
and Australia, New Zealand and South Africa
and distributed in the United States of America
by Heinemann, a division of Reed Elsevier Inc.
361 Hanover Street, Portsmouth, New Hampshire NH 03801 3959

Can't Stand Up for Falling Down first published by Methuen in 1991
Copyright © 1991 Richard Cameron
Pond Life copyright © 1992 Richard Cameron
The Mortal Ash copyright © 1994 Richard Cameron
All of You Mine copyright © 1997 Richard Cameron

Introduction and collection copyright © 1998 Richard Cameron

The author has asserted his moral rights

ISBN 0-413-71660-0

A CIP catalogue record for this book is available from the British Library

Typeset by Deltatype Ltd, Birkenhead, Merseyside
Printed and bound in Great Britain by
Cox & Wyman Ltd, Reading, Berkshire

Caution

Contents

Richard Cameron:
A Chronology

1985 *Haunted Sunflowers* (retitled *Handle with Care*) performed at the National Student Drama Festival

1988 *Strugglers* performed at the National Student Drama Festival

1989 *The Moon's the Madonna* performed at the National Student Drama Festival and Battersea Arts Centre, London

1990 *Can't Stand Up for Falling Down* performed at the National Student Drama Festival, Edinburgh Festival and at the Hampstead Theatre, London

1992 *Pond Life* performed at the Bush Theatre, London, in association with the Royal National Theatre Studio

1993 *Not Fade Away* performed at the Bush Theatre

1994 *The Mortal Ash* performed at the Bush Theatre
    Almost Grown performed at the Royal National Theatre, London
    Seven performed at the Birmingham Rep.

1995 *With Every Beat* performed at the West Yorkshire Playhouse
    Stone Scissors Paper BBC television play

1996 *In Bed with Billy Cotton* performed at the Belgrade Theatre, Coventry
    All of You Mine performed at the Bush Theatre

Introduction

These plays are all set in South Yorkshire because that's where I'm from and I like to write about what I know. Place is almost the first thing I think about when I start to work on a play. In *Can't Stand Up for Falling Down* it's a two or three mile stretch of the river Don. In *Pond Life* it's a hole in the ground near Stainforth. *The Mortal Ash* came about when an old tree-lined quarry and lake – in the same stretch of the river Don – became the scene of local outrage when it began to be filled with hospital and veterinary waste. *All of You Mine* began with a visit to a garden centre on the slag heap of an old pit, and it was the coal tubs filled with flowers in the car park that set me off with a story.

The language of South Yorkshire to me has a rhythm and a poetry to it, which cuts corners and is full of alliteration. That, and the fact that I like to work through characters who like to keep their gobs shut – see all say nowt – is both a challenge and a joy to explore.

Can't Stand Up for Falling Down is a relatively early play. I look back on its style and language now, its cross-over weaving of a story, and wonder how on earth I ever did it. I remember that the writing came in a two week burst after several weeks of thinking about it.

I distinctly remember, when I began work on *The Mortal Ash*, deciding I'd like to try a classic three-act structure – and believing it to be a fairly painless, straightforward way of organizing plot. Now I know better. How long to keep something buried before a character reveals is a tough task, as is weaving in clues that don't stand out in neon. However that process I found fascinating, even if it did take forever.

The weeks of working out structure are both a torture and a joy – but I've learnt enough now to know that to start writing without knowing where you're going only leads you into a cul-de-sac around seven eighths of the way through. I usually begin writing when the notes I've made need both hands to carry around the house.

Richard Cameron
August 1997

Can't Stand Up for Falling Down

Characters

Lynette, *twenty-two*
Ruby, *twenty-six*
Jodie, *eighteen*

We also see them, through their memory, eight years ago.

The characters of:
Carl, *Ruby's son*
Elaine, *Ruby's sister*
Martine, *hairdresser*
Bernice, *hairdresser*
are played by the three women.

The play is set in the Don Valley, South Yorkshire.

Can't Stand Up for Falling Down was first performed at
the Edinburgh Fringe Festival in 1990 and then at the
Hampstead Theatre, London, in November of that year
with the following cast:

Lynette	Joanne Wootton
Ruby	Deborah Kilner
Jodie	Donna Stones

Directed by Richard Cameron
Set and lighting by Lizz Poulter
Sound by Emma McBride
Company Manager Ruth Thomas
Stage Management Kate Brook, Nigel Anstow, Sarah Jenkin

Then. Eight years ago. Summer. A river valley.

Lynette I dropped down in the grass. Heard it like an Indian, coming through the earth, high up over the other side, coming up the lane to the top on the other side then winding down through the trees to the river and our bridge. Ringing loud like it was right here and then soft like it had gone into a hole in the ground and out again, nearer, louder, going through tunnels in the trees. I don't want it to be for us. Don't make it for us.

I see my mother in my head, back at the cottage, counting the roses on the walls, the tassels on the lamp by her bed. Dad must have run up the hill to the village. And she, waiting, crying in pain again, thinking of me in the field, fourteen, racing up the track to swing the gate open for them, worried. But I didn't. I lay down hard so it wouldn't see me and wished it away and even when it didn't come over our bridge and I knew it wasn't coming over the bridge, I still thought it would. They've gone down the wrong track. They'll stop and come back. Trying to trick me. Make me feel happy that it's for somebody else so I won't feel so bad when it turns out to be for us.

But it didn't come back. It kept on going and away, along the far side of the river, and I counted the quarries till I couldn't hear it any more. And I thought if it's for us, guide them back, don't be so cruel if you know it's for us.

But they didn't come back. Even when I knew it wasn't hers, I thought it was, and wouldn't let myself smile or laugh yet, like I wanted to, knowing I knew it was for someone else. Soon as I REALLY knew, I knew I would be laughing. I wouldn't be able to stop myself from being happy that someone else was ill, and I knew God would punish me and think me bad but I didn't care. I would fall out of a tree and break my leg and it would kill me and God would say, 'Serves you right for laughing at someone else's ambulance'. But I didn't care.

And then they came back and YES it climbed the side of the hill away from the river, though the trees, tunnels of trees, ringing loud and soft and away from me, over the top of the valley, away from ME, up now, crying and laughing in the field, dancing because it was someone else's ambulance and not my mother's. And I'm picking flowers for her, and I can see her when I give them to her and she's trimming and filling the vase and singing softly to herself.

Ruby I knew for sure the day before Al Janney died.

Aunt Madge said so. I wanted to ask her about it, but didn't. We sat in her little back room by the window, the table full of brasses that I dulled and she polished, and after a while of me thinking how I was going to tell her, she said,
'Does your mother know?'
and I said 'Does my mother know what?'
and she said 'Getting yourself pregnant'
and I said, 'Who says I am?'
and she said 'Aren't you?'

And I dulled a little brass ship and said 'Don't tell' and she said 'I won't if you don't want me to.'

I told her what I could and my fear went away and came on again in waves, but mostly I thanked God to have someone to talk to and whilst we talked I dulled and she polished. She asked me who it was and I couldn't tell her. Not before I told him. Tomorrow I'd tell him.

It was the Saturday that Al died. The day I went to tell Royce, when I was eighteen and expecting his baby and I had to ask him what I should do and I walked to their shop and just before I got there, I turned off, back along Church Lane and round, and on our road again, and past our house and up to the shop and turned off the other way and Saturday morning I walked miles to get to their shop up the road and when I got there it was closed for dinner.

Al was looking in the window. He had a little girl with him. I went down the alley to the back of the shop, up the yard and I could hear the radio playing in the back room.

John Farrow, Kite and Royce were playing cards and drinking beer. He laid a card and looked at me and the look said enough to make me want to go, and it was his turn to lay again and I turned away and he said 'Come here' and I came to him and stood by his chair and his hand went between my knees and stroked the front of my leg where they all could see.
'Don't', I said, and tried to pull away, but his hand held me fast and they smiled.
'Get us three pasties,' he said, and his hand that held me went into his back pocket and he put the money in my hand. I turned to go and he patted my behind.

I went to the butchers and got them. Al and the little girl were still at Royce's shop front. He was flapping the letter box. I went up to tell him to go but Royce opened the door and swore at him and pushed him away. I gave Royce the bag and said 'See you tonight,' and as he took the bag Al dodged into the shop. Royce went in and tried to chase him out, cursing.

And I walked home.

Jodie We never did more than hold hands, me and Al Janney. There was only ever one kiss. I thought I was grown up. I was ten and he was a lot older than me. I knew he was different. I knew he was still a boy in a man's body.

I was in love with him. It was our secret. No-one to know and tell me I couldn't go around with a boy who was gone in the head, no-one to tell me it was wrong. But it wasn't wrong. We were happy. It went on forever, like the river. Time was slow and easy and measured in laughing and smiles and dandelion clocks and in Al Janney's eyes, and there was no before or after in it to look back on and say 'we were happy then', it was ALL now, and it was ALL happy.

We were married in May. I had the cotton and Al had all his pockets full of all the sweet papers from all the streets in town, and down we went to our hollow in the hill above the river and tied the sweet papers to the branches of our secret tree, and so it became like sacred. And we laid bluebells on our altar stone, under what we said was our stained glass windows that were dancing in the sunlight and I said I would love honour and obey him as long as we both shall live amen and he said it to me and we drank pretend wine from our silver paper cups . . . and then he kissed me.

Ruby Sometimes it had felt good when Royce showed me off in front of his friends. And their eyes when his hands were on me! And they would laugh embarrassed and I was becoming a woman and we knew things about love they didn't.

Walking home that Saturday afternoon I knew it wouldn't happen again because NOW I was a woman and somehow my secret of what was inside me wanted to make secret and private everything that was me and Royce, and I was unhappy because I knew it wouldn't happen, and I knew it couldn't be me and Royce and the baby, because there was my family and his family and his life and his friends, and I cried because I had given him a bag of pasties and a baby and he wasn't the kind of man to say 'thank you' for either.

Jodie That Saturday afternoon we went for a walk along the river bank. We sat watching the barges. Three men came towards us. They had two dogs. The dogs went down the bank for rats and slopped along the water's edge and came up again, dripping. Al saw who it was and said 'come on' to me and I looked and saw it was Royce Boland from the shop and two others. He had a big gun and I thought they must be after rats or rabbits. Al was up and walking off fast and said 'come on' to me again without looking back and I jumped up and caught him up and we walked fast and daren't turn round. Al must have thought they were after him, after they punched him in the shop and pushed and kicked him between them, and I nearly stumbled, we were almost breaking into a run, and Al said, 'It's them men'.

And now we were running and he held my hand to keep me with him and I looked back and they were running too and shouting and making the dogs bark and I felt some sick come up and sting my throat.

Lynette I give her the flowers for still being here, and go out to Dad who's working the lock gates for a barge coming down. I'm happy because the bell wasn't ringing for her and she liked the flowers, but Dad is not happy and when I ask why, he doesn't say, so I don't know if it's mother or me, or something else. And then he says 'youths messing about' and I understand, and think of the boy who they dared to walk across the weir for sixpence who slipped on the green slime in just an inch of summer water rolling over the weir top. Up went his legs and he crashed down hard and shot into the swirling suds and under, whirling in the strong currents, twisting and taking him away underneath while they waited by the weir for him to come up again and waited till they knew he wouldn't and ran the bank and the bridge and the other bank and both banks till they knew and went away and told the police who searched and searched and for seven days the town waited while men watched the river, but they missed him, and the next day his blue and bloated body popped up outside the power station, six miles downstream.

My father was one of the boys who dared him to cross the weir. So now he works the lock gates and respects the river and watches, and shouts at youths messing about who call him an old misery and laugh and swear at him from the far bank, but they don't know the dangers like him, and he gets sad sometimes, like now, because he was once upon a time a boy, and remembers how good it was, and how dangerous . . . and isn't now.

And I think of the ambulance again, and look down at the water rushing from the chamber, look in my head for a drowned boy, stepped between a gun and a rat . . . and Dad has made me sad.

Jodie Al could run like a rabbit but he had hold of me and I was only ten and I couldn't run any faster and holding his hand I was stumbling. Then a narrow bit of the path came up and we had to let go and I had to run behind him and he was getting further away from me. We were running up to the bridge and the road. I daren't look back. Al was at the fence by the bridge now and up, standing on the top, shouting. The dogs were nearly up to me. Then Al was down and up again with stones, throwing them at the dogs as I climbed the slope to the fence. And he was holding me as I jumped down into the road.

Ruby I knew what I was. I didn't need anyone else to tell me. Speaks for itself, pregnant at eighteen. Walking round the streets and round again to get home that afternoon I tried real hard to feel as bad as I could, telling myself all the bad I had done, all the bad that was going to happen, thinking that if I brought it all into my head NOW and cried, and MADE myself bad, something . . . I don't know . . . something might be waiting at the other end with some goodness in it. Something to tell me everything was going to be all right in the end, even when it seemed everything was all wrong, something to show me it was worth going through all this, that everything was going to be all right.

Jodie The black dog started to push through the fence. Al swung his boot to hit it in the side but it saw, and pulled back so he caught it hard on the cheekbone and it howled and went back to Royce who was shouting swearwords, running towards us with one of the other two. The third one wasn't there. He must have run up the hill to cut us off at the top.

Ruby And suddenly Al came into my head, and how we used to make fun of him, taunt him, and him so daft and simple and laughing and desperate for someone to be his friend that he'd do anything for you. Like once Royce said they'd got him to lick up dog dirt before they'd let him play. I don't know if it's true – Royce has told me lots of stories – but we must have made his life a hell, and now I was thinking of him and thinking of what I'd done to him, and how I thought him a fool, and what laughs he'd given us.

Jodie I'm running again. 'Wait. Wait for me Al!' He's a long way in front and leaving me. Royce and the other one are at the fence, and somewhere above us, cutting us off by the road that doubles back up the side of the hill, is the third one. Royce calls to him and his shout comes back through the trees and Al switches to the other side of the road and I see he's heading for the track that follows the river upstream, past the weir, to the quarries.

Ruby And now, suddenly, in a rush, I loved him. A wave of his goodness and my cruelty washed over me, and thinking it all out was making me feel bad, like I wanted, and I kept it going and made myself remember . . . how I'd kissed him, how with Royce and the others we'd told him what to do with a girl and how I would show him and he came up to me and closed his eyes for ages and we fell about laughing and then I kissed him and Royce put Al's hands on me and I put my arms around him and pulled him to me and he must have been holding his breath because he pulled away gasping and red and we all laughed, but I knew I'd shown him something, felt his body shudder against mine, knew he was a child in a man's body.

And as I remembered, I thought how bad, how evil I was, and still am, and deserve it all, every bad thing coming.

And then I knew that it was helping me, that I WOULD get to the other end, because I knew now that when I got home I was going to tell my mother about the baby. There would be hell in the house but it would be all right, because I deserved it. It would be all right . . . because I deserved it . . . because of Al Janney.

Jodie Royce caught my hair and lifted me off my feet and then I was on the floor and thinking they were going to shoot me, head in the dust, my knees under me, begging them not to hurt me. And they pulled me up, made me stand up, and said, 'Make him come back. Scream. Go on', and so I screamed. 'Louder'. And I screamed louder and I could see Al a long way off so I screamed long and loud like they were killing me and I was crying and screaming and crying because Al was still running and they MIGHT have been killing me for all he knew.

Ruby And when I got home I told my mother, because Al had made me, but it didn't happen like I wanted it to. She wasn't angry and screaming at me, 'You whore!' and packing my bags and Dad didn't get up and whack me. It was long, unbearable thinking silences that I didn't deserve when I wanted to be punished for what I was and what I'd done. She was wanting to help me and helping me made me feel worse and unworthy of her help. And yet . . . this feeling worse . . . as it was digging in to me, somehow it was scouring out all the dirt, and I DID know that everything could be all right even when it wasn't, and there was so much dirt in me, but she didn't mind, and I knew how much I loved her then, for the way she was cleaning me out, like the thousands of days of pots and pans, she kept on cleaning us out, making our hearts shine, knowing they'd only get used and bruised and black again, but she didn't mind.

I loved her, and Dad, and Al Janney, and Aunt Madge, who also spent her life shining brasses and hearts and in the middle of all my badness I knew there was something else, something good, because there were good people around me, and I wasn't alone, and my baby would be shown some love.

Jodie I watched them go along the track and followed them. They went into the first quarry and sent the dogs to find him. Royce snapped the gun together, brought it to his shoulder and fired at the quarry face. The bang came back to me loud like thunder cracking and a swarm of jackdaws flew out and wheeled away over the top. Al wasn't there. The dogs knew.

Lynette I waved the barge downstream, the dead boy and the ambulance still waiting in my head for me to turn round and look back at the lock and upstream to the weir and quarries. But I wouldn't.

Jodie They went into the second quarry. Two shots went into the quarry face. Royce sat on a rock and smoked a cigarette whilst the other two clambered about with the dogs. Al wasn't here.

Lynette I looked instead across the river, up the side of the valley to the clump of trees with the little hollow, where I found a tree that day with the sweet papers and the flat stone and knew it was a secret child's church that I had found, and left it untouched. I left it alone for the child to come back and play and pray.

Jodie They went in to the last quarry, the biggest, canyon high, blasted rocks as big as houses against the cliff, higher than the sun. And the gun shots boomed into the cliff and boomed back, deafening, splitting and rolling in the air, as though a shower of rocks should fall with it, and the dogs hunted and the three men climbed and called and peered into caves between the fallen boulders, working their way around from one end of the quarry to the other, and I prayed that they wouldn't find him. Please God.

Lynette And I wondered if she was there now, praying on the side of the hill, and would she mind if I, here, prayed with her for a while, to keep the good things in my life strong and clear, and the bad thoughts, the daydreams and nightmares waiting to throw a blanket over me and carry me away, dark inside and screaming – keep them down and locked away. Please God.

Jodie Then I saw Al come out like a rabbit and make for the quarry face at the far end, and then they all saw him. The dogs barked and scrambled after him and the three men worked their way across the boulders towards him, calling, shouting, laughing, knowing he had nowhere to go. Then he started to climb, away from the dogs, fast at first, in a panic rush to get above them, then more slowly, stretching, moving into a steady climb, then more slowly still, as he went higher and higher, inching up and across, up and across, and they just stood and watched, and waited, and shouted, making him go on and higher in fear of them, a long time, until he was stopped and could go no further and just clung to the rock, high above them.

And I ran into the quarry and begged them to leave him. Please. He can't hang on any longer. He's stuck. Help him. And they laughed and waited and I kept saying please help him and then I think they got scared because he was stuck high up there and they didn't know what to do, so they pretended to be bored and went away with the dogs and left us.

Ruby Tonight I am going to tell Royce about the baby, and I won't be scared of what he says.

Jodie He was too frightened to move.

Ruby I am not scared. Al Janney has taught me not to be frightened.

Jodie And then he fell.

Ruby It CAN be all right, deep down, even when things are all wrong.

Lynette Please God, I prayed, keep the good things

coming. And it felt good that maybe a little girl was praying the same prayer as me across the river in her little secret church. And I was fourteen and needed a little secret church of my own, for there were things I still needed to know. Like would there always be joy and dread in my life? Will all my days have happiness and sadness together? Can there be one without the other? Can we know one without the other?

And the little girl, whoever she was, had made me happy again.

Now. A suggestion of interiors superimposed over 'then'.

Ruby (*to audience*) When I told Royce about the baby he told me he would stay with me and we'd get engaged if I went and said the father was somebody else. (*Pause.*) I wouldn't do it. (*Pause.*) But I wouldn't say it was Royce's either, not if he didn't want. So he left me. And then the rumours started, about me carrying Al Janney's baby and I suppose Royce must have started them, and in a way it was partly my fault that they spread because I wouldn't say who the father was, except it wasn't Al's, until the whole town decided I was carrying Al's baby. I thought Royce would come back to me, you see, if I said nothing, but he didn't.

And in all that time I never gave a thought to what Al's parents must be going through. I never thought. I was too bothered about me and the baby and losing Royce. I didn't want my baby to have a dead father so I said nothing and waited for Royce to come back to me. But he didn't.

I had a boy. Carl. He's seven now. I got so I wanted to see

Al Janney's parents to try to explain to them, and maybe say how much he meant to me when he was alive, and how he still means something special to me now. But by the time I felt I had the courage to see them, they left town and I never got the chance. Now they were gone, away from it all, trying to start a new life and I was part of their reason for going. And I am part of the reason for his mother coming back and doing what she did. I must be.

I'm not married. I want to be. I'm seeing a man at the moment – but it's complicated. When isn't it? Maybe it's my punishment. They say it all comes back to you, don't they? I just want someone to be with me, to love me. But the men I get don't want that. Maybe it's Carl that scares them away.

We hear **Carl** *and* **Elaine**, **Ruby**'s *sister, arrive in the house, somewhere offstage.* **Carl** *is shouting for his mother.*

You can't come in yet! Don't come in here. Either of you. Carl, don't let Aunty Elaine come in, I'm wrapping her present.

Carl (*off*) Mum says you can't go in.

Elaine (*off*) Oh, all right.

Carl (*off*) Can I come in?

Ruby No, not yet. Wait in the front room till I get organised.

Carl (*off*) Why can't I come in?

Ruby Because I've got you a present as well.

Carl (*off*) What?

Elaine (*off*) Come on, do as you're told.

Carl (*off*) It's not my birthday. Do I get a present on your birthday?

Elaine (*off*) Looks like it. You're spoilt.

Ruby (*to us*) He's been pestering me for weeks to get him a fishing rod.

And so there I am this morning in Royce's shop. (*Pause.*) That must have been his wife.

Lynette *appears in the shop.*

Right. Present done. Get the dinner on. Take Carl back to school in the car then off to meet the man of the moment. With complications.

She goes off with the present and the fishing rod.

Lynette (*to us*) My mother died seven years ago, when I was fifteen. Dad got finished with the waterways. We had to give up the lock-keeper's cottage and moved into a council house in town. I got a job in the coal board offices. I met Royce Boland through going to their shop every Friday night for Dad, to get him his bait for fishing on Saturdays. He still goes to the river. Never catches anything. I don't think there's much in it now.

Royce was three years older than me. We went to a few dances. I was married to him at eighteen. He didn't want me working, so I finished. I work in the shop now, sometimes.

We don't have any children.

I don't get out much, except for my walks. I used to go to my mother's Pentecostal church, but it wasn't worth the rows, so I don't go now. I miss it in a way.

We hear **Royce** *arrive in the back, whistling, moving through the house.* **Lynette** *hears, moves back a little from 'his chair' and waits. The whistling comes into the room. Stops.* **Lynette** *waits for him to sit.*

It's ready. (*Pause.*) Shepherd's pie. (*She goes off to fetch his meal, returning with it on a tray.*)

Do you want the chair? (*She gets a chair and places the tray on it, in front of him, then moves back, watching him from a distance.*)

Did you have to speak to me like you did? With people in the shop? (*Pause.*) I'm not starting anything, I'm only saying. (*Pause.*) I don't want to be humiliated in front of other people. (*Pause.*) She knew, she must have heard. (*Pause.*) I don't care whether you eat it or not. It doesn't smell of bleach. What, do you think I'm trying to poison you? You must have a guilty conscience. (*She ducks suddenly, in response to him about to throw something at her. Pause. She starts to cry.*)

I'm not crying. I'm not frightened of you. Yes, I bleached the sink this morning. (*Sniffs her hands.*) It's on my hands still, yes. (*Pause.*) It's not on your dinner.

She gets up, moves over to smell the dinner. Sniffs. As she is coming up, her head is pushed violently down into the dinner. She is struggling, her face in the plate. Eventually she is released, stands, wipes the dinner from her face, moving away. She watches him get up and move off.

Yes, go on, sleep it off.

She picks up the tray, goes off. Comes back with a newspaper and a dressing table set and a shopping bag. She wraps the pieces of the set in newspaper and puts them in the bag.

I've started taking this with me when I go out of the house. When I go for a walk. I don't want to leave it. Not with him still in the house. It was my mother's. It's the only thing I have to remember her by. (*Pause.*) I must be mad. Twenty-two and walking the streets with a dressing table set. (*Pause.*) No, I don't walk the streets. I go where I know I can get away from people. I go down by the river.

She finishes packing the set, picks up the bag and goes.

Jodie *appears at 'her workplace'.*

Jodie It's as if a whole chunk has been taken out of my memory. There's just a gap. I'm told I was in hospital, then at home in bed all summer and I should have started at the secondary school when everybody else did in the September, but I didn't. I wouldn't talk. And then when I did start school I wouldn't work and they thought I might have to go to a special school. I can't remember any of it.

I think I know how I got better, because now I can see that there was a time when Al was all my life and then since, a time when he hasn't been anywhere in my mind at all. In between I think I must have been cancelling him out of my brain – that to be better I had not just to forget him – in the way your mother tells you to forget a boy who's broken your heart, but to REALLY forget him altogether, as though the memory was rubbed out. And somehow, with the help of everyone else, who never asked me about him, I made it work and he became no more than an old toy that goes in the attic and out of your mind.

And when I used to see Royce Boland afterwards, I knew he'd come from some bad dream I once had. But it wasn't real and I was growing up and taking my place in the real world.

And today I find out about Al Janney's mother, and it all comes back. And I get such an awful feeling about Royce Boland, I'm standing in his shop! What did I think I was going to say to him? Or do?

I work in a hairdressers at the moment. Just a backstreet one, nothing fancy. There's four of us and the manageress, but she's never there. There's Bernice and Martine – they're both married, though to hear them you wouldn't think so – and there's Tim. He's just started. He's a bit shy.

Bernice Jodie, come on, we're off.

Jodie I think I'll give it a miss, Bernice, if you don't mind, I don't fancy going for a drink.

Bernice Martine?

Martine What?

Bernice She says she's not coming. (*To* **Jodie**.) Just have a coffee, then, that's all I'm having.

Martine What are you doing, then?

Jodie I don't know.

Bernice Come on, Jodie, come with us, it's Friday.

Martine We're going to that pub we went to, by the river.

Bernice The boat.

Martine They do nice meals.

Bernice I'm not having a meal.

Martine Why not?

Bernice I'm too fat. Look at all this.

Martine You're not fat. (*To* **Jodie**.) Is she?

Jodie No.

Bernice I am compared to you.

Martine Well that's because I'm tall, isn't it? I only look thin. If I was as small as you, I'd be as fat as you.

Bernice Thanks.

Martine Come on, Jodie.

Jodie All right.

They go.

Ruby Usually I meet him in the car park at the pub by the river. He gets in my car and I drive us over the bridge and down the track to the quarries . . . we have a place where we stop. I told him I didn't want to go today. The police might still be around. I didn't want to go even if they weren't. Instead we went for a walk along the river bank, along this side.

He's married. I didn't find out until we'd been seeing one another for a month. Then he begged me to forgive him and said it was all finished between him and her anyway, and she was seeing someone else. And I believed him.

It was a mistake walking up this way. You can see the quarries across the river. He wants me to sit down, but I won't. He wants to know what's wrong, and I won't tell him – because I don't know myself, exactly.

Lynette There's my name somewhere here . . . here it is. Lynette. I scratched it on this bridge when I was twelve. And somewhere . . . I can't remember where – I did find it once – are my Dad's initials that he did when he was about the same age. (*Moves away.*) Is it on this side?

Jodie I think it's thinking about Mrs Janney that's put me in this mood. I shouldn't have come with them, talking about men all the time. It gets a bit much after a while, a bit crude. They tease Tim something awful, talking about sex, making him embarrassed. No wonder he's off work. I'm sure it gets to him.

Ruby And we walk back to my car, and he wants to know what's wrong. (*To him.*) Nothing, honestly, there isn't anything. (*To us.*) And then I'm telling him, and it's as if I'm not there, like I'm outside of myself, listening, as if I'm already at home, telling my sister Elaine what I said.

(*To him.*) This isn't the way I want things to be between us, but nothing's changed. (*Pause.*) You say it will, but it won't. You let me start to think too much about you. I want to be with you but we have to meet like this. I want more, but I can't have more, can I? (*Pause.*) I don't want to wait for you. (*Pause.*) Because you have a wife who loves you – she does! And if we stay like this, one day for sure she will find out, and I don't want that. (*Pause.*) You tricked me. (*Pause.*) Yes you did. You let me think I was taking over from what you told me was finished. It won't ever be, will it? (*Pause.*) I just woke up today. (*Pause.*)

Nothing's brought this on (*To us.*) except Al Janney and Mrs Janney and Royce Boland. (*To him.*) I just woke up today. You've led me into all this and for you it's an easy game – just finish work early, a couple of hours with Ruby and home for tea. You don't even have to put any extra miles on the clock, and no risk of your wife finding anything on the back seat, we do it in my car!

Jodie How is it that some people don't get any wiser as they get older? How can they say such stupid things? I don't like people making fun of other people just because they're different.

(*To* **Martine**.) Why can't you leave people alone to be what they want to be? He can't help what he is.

Martine Shut up, then, keep your voice down. I'm only having a bit of fun. What's the matter with you?

Jodie I don't think it's right, making fun like that.

Martine I don't mean it. (*To* **Bernice**.) Tell her.

Bernice She doesn't mean it. Don't take it so personal.

Martine Look, love, I think the world of that boy. Tim's a smashing lad.

Jodie Then why don't you tell him, then? Why do you say all the things you say to him? Why keep going on about what he is?

Martine I don't know.

Jodie Why don't you tell him you think he's a smashing lad?

Martine I don't know. We can't always say what we want to say, can we?

Bernice He knows we don't mean what we say.

Jodie He doesn't know! Why should he know?

Martine He can see through US, can't he? I'm just a daft

old sod, I don't mean any harm. Underneath we're just
. . . well . . . It's all talk, isn't it? (*Pause*.) Jodie . . . what
you said . . . I'm not. I'm not sex mad.

Martine It's just something to talk about. Put a bit of
spice in life.

Bernice She'd run a mile, wouldn't you?

Martine I would. I've never been with anybody else but
my Tony. That's God's truth. Never. And that's the way I
want it to stay.

Jodie I'm sorry.

Bernice What are we having, then, same again? (*Moves
off.*)

Jodie And when she'd gone for the drinks, Martine told
me about Bernice's fella. It wasn't a man. It was her son,
David. He was ten. He was a little mongol boy. She'd let
me say all those things and she never said. That was who
she was with when she was out with her fella, taking him
ice skating, bowling, Martine said. Why didn't she say?
She let me say all that and she never said. What do I say
for her?

Ruby (*to us*) I don't know whether I was doing the right
thing or not, but I had to end it. (*To him*.) I think we'd
better finish. (*To us*.) And I can hear Elaine saying to me,
'What did he say when you said that?' and I tell her. 'He
kept saying "No" over and over, "Please Ruby, I need
you, stay with me"' and she's laughing and saying, 'He
didn't say that, did he?'

But I want him out. I want him out and me crying. I want
him gone and me miserable again. And I tell him to go.
But he doesn't want to go, and I don't want him to go in a
way . . . but I don't want to be in the back seat of a car all
my life!

Lynette And seeing the river again, slow, sure, and deep, pass under me and on, past where our little cottage was, but isn't now – they've knocked it down – it's all right, I'm happy. The river will always be here, passing through. And it gives me strength.

I love God, and I still pray, and I know that all of this between Royce and me will pass; that things will get better, or they will get worse, but they will PASS, because this is the life I am made to live, and when God is ready to change things, he will. And all that I have to do is keep going, keep praying, see the good in people and in things around me. Like here. There is good here. There is God here . . . and my mother in my shopping bag . . . and I'm happy again.

Jodie I've been seeing Tim a bit, at night, now and then. Just out for a drink. Things are a lot better at work. They still talk about fellas . . . and what they'd like to do to them . . . you know . . . but I can understand it better now – and Tim gets them going, because he joins in as bad as them! They're not sure how to deal with it, but it's their fun, and we do all seem to be easier with one another.

Tim and me go to the pub by the river on Sundays. It's a bit of a habit now. Summer evenings. It's nice, along the river bank . . . my river bank. (*Pause.*) It's like the child I was is another person, someone else that I was very close to but she went away somewhere.

I wake up some mornings after she's been in my dreams, and for a few minutes she's very close, and sometimes she brings Al Janney with her, and she's still there sometimes when I get up and I can sort of see her in the mirror under my skin but by the time I'm at the bottom of the stairs she's gone, and I'm me again.

Last Sunday we walked back from the pub and it was just getting dark when we were crossing the bridge. I could see somebody leaning over. I thought they were thinking of jumping in at first, but then I could see it was a woman and she had this bag and it must have been full of broken bits of crockery or glass because you could hear it when she rattled about bringing pieces out. And then we saw that she was dropping the pieces, a few at a time, into the river, and she was singing to herself.

Ruby I'm making Carl the only man in my life. This summer I'm spending as much time with him as I can. I'm going to get myself a job for this month, while he's still at school, try and earn myself a bit to put towards a week's holiday, maybe two if I save enough. Get a caravan. Spend all day on the beach, in the arcades, let him do some fishing – no, he won't do that. He's been ONCE with that rod I bought him. Elaine's husband, Robert, took him. All day they were gone. Never caught a thing, either of them. He's lost interest now. Rob's offered to take him again but he won't go.

I want to be with him this summer. I want him to have a good holiday. Something for him to remember. I want it to be something I'll remember. He won't be young for ever.

I feel that I've lost too much of him in a way . . . time's gone by and he was there, and I could have been there with him, just BEEN there, watching him be four, five, six . . . and instead I feel it's gone and I was too busy trying to be myself, too busy finding out what I wanted, thinking I wanted a man, thinking it would all be happy families if we had a man in the house, but we didn't have, so it couldn't be happy, and Carl, my son, you were left to make the best of it and grow up on your own, whilst your mother got herself deeper into a pathetic, pathetic state.

Well, it's gone now. I learnt something about being a mother the day Mrs Janney joined her son, after eight years of not watching him grow up. I can't begin to understand that fall, but I learnt something from it: fill my days with Carl while I can, and make NOW what matters.

Lynette Royce has now moved into the back bedroom, thank God. It's been a bit of a time, these last few weeks. I got a knife on the bedroom door lock and managed to get the paint off so it works, I can lock it at night now. Makes it a bit safer. I just don't know what he might do next, after the things he's said to me. Coming in, throwing things. Spoiling things in the house. What's the point of trying to keep things nice? I keep my room clean, I make my own meals when he's out. It's like a pigsty down there.

I tried to clean it up after he'd pulled everything out of the kitchen cupboard and smashed it, but I cut my hand quite bad on a bit of glass from the sauce bottle, I think it was, and I had to leave it. I should have had stitches really. It's funny, I thought it was tomato ketchup.

'Serves you fucking right,' he says. 'Cleaning up. You're always cleaning up. Leave it. Fucking LEAVE IT!' and something's exploded in my head and he must have hit my ear. My hand's full of blood but it's my ear that hurts. 'Don't you swear in this house! You stop saying your foul language to me, I won't have it. Don't swear!' and I'm hanging on to the edge of the sink to stop from falling over, I'm going dizzy. It makes me ill to hear bad words said before God and he knows it and he says it all the more, over and over, and my hand's under the tap and my head's swimming and ringing loud and the water turns red.

That night, I mend the door lock with one hand, while my other hand is throbbing through the cloth, and I hear him hammering and sawing in the shed in the yard, like it's been for days now into the night, but I don't care any

more about what he's doing, I don't care, and I don't care
if God doesn't want me to say it, I wish he were dead. I
wish he were dead.

Jodie I've got another fella. Tim knows all about him. He
doesn't mind. Well, he's not really my boyfriend, is he?
We're just mates. No, this fella, I really love. Trouble is,
he loves somebody else – Bernice. I'm in love with
Bernice's little boy, David. He's smashing. I went to their
school fête, had a really good time. The kids were so
happy, so loving, so full of life. I had to put my head
through a board and have wet sponges thrown at me, and
I had a go on this stall throwing at cups and plates, seeing
how many you could smash. I won a teddy. They have so
many problems, some of the children, but they were still
happy. I couldn't believe it. It was catching. It was a
really lovely, happy day.

I want to marry David but he's in love with his Mum.

Lynette One night I didn't hear him come in the house.
I'd just had a bath and was getting ready for bed, putting
on my nightdress and he was stood in the doorway,
watching me. I waited, and said 'I want to go to bed', and
he said, 'Come on, then'.

'Don't come near me.' I could smell the drink and
cigarettes and he held my shoulders. When I tried to get
away he pushed me down, landing me heavy on the bed
and my hand was under me and it felt like it was bleeding
again and I said it was but he wouldn't get up, just
fumbled around and tore my nightdress at the top and I
was just saying, 'please, don't, please, no' and I couldn't
move because it was hurting my hand. And then I had his
hair in my good hand and somehow pulled him aside and
got out from under him, and up, and he was too fat and
drunk to get to me before I got out and into the bathroom
and locked myself in and yes my hand was bleeding
again.

And I was a bitch, he said, and I had got a lover, and that's who I saw when I went for my walks, I was meeting somebody.

'You're a dirty bitch. And you can go to him, I don't care. I know you wait for him down by the river. I know you're laid on your back in the grass. I hope he gets more out of you than I ever had. You couldn't do it right when I first had you and you're no better now. I've had better women before you and I've had better women since. Do you think you were the first? Eh? EH? I'll tell you. I've got a son seven years old. And I've been seeing his mother ever since and she'd take me back right now if I wanted. If I wanted to. So I don't need you. It's like laying in bed with a fucking stick insect!'

'Go to her then,' I said. 'Go on. If she'll take you. Get out and go to her. Go on, get out!'

Pause.

And he went into my room and I heard something smash against the wall and smash again and it must have been the dressing table set and it smashed again and I wanted to be in our cottage by the river with Dad eating his tea that Mum had shown me how to cook for him and she was pleased and proud and happy, and Dad was hungry and happy and didn't know I'd made it and we were bursting to tell him and we were bursting because we were happy and GOD, WHY? WHY? I want to be there again.

Jodie I didn't see where he came from. He was just there, right next to me, with David coming up the grass bank in front of me, pulling the cart. And I looked to see if there were other people in the park because he looked a bit mad in the eyes and there was only a group of young boys round the other side of the pond.

David was laughing because he'd just gone a long way fast down the hill and now he was nearly up to me to do it again and Royce said, 'Where did you get that from?' 'He was given it,' I said, and I thought, I know you, Royce Boland, I know you, but you don't know me, you don't remember me, and you can't scare me any more.

'I made that for my son, not for that spastic,' he said, and then went down in big strides to David coming up, not laughing now, and grabbed the rope, and I ran down and caught the rope before he could pull it away and David was frightened by this big man with wild eyes and he sat down, screaming. I didn't say anything. I just held on, and he was pulling me back up the hill till he could see I wasn't going to let go. Then he turned and stopped and let go and I fell and the cart spun and crashed on me and he said, 'Get that taken back to where it came from. Give it back. You'd better give it back.' And then turned and walked off, fast.

I got David and the cart up the hill and we sat on the bench. David was soon all right again but I was angry. Angry that it had happened and that it was Royce Boland and he had tried to make me scared but I wasn't going to let him make me cry any more and I was going to get him. Some way I was going to get him.

Ruby It was going to be our summer together, but I couldn't get a job and I couldn't take him on holiday. Elaine offered to take him with them for a fortnight but I said no. Then I had to say yes because of all this with

Royce. I had to get Carl out of the way of it all. And now I had to get Royce to stop what he was doing to us.

First, he just turned up one night, about three weeks ago, wanting to see Carl, trying to tell me he wanted to take him out – father and son. Said he was sorry for everything, for everything that had happened, and all I could say was NO. And he said, 'I'm his father, I want to see him,' and I said, 'You're not his father. He doesn't even know who you are. Why now, after eight years? Just go home and stay away from us'. I managed to shut the door on him and waited for him to start banging again but he went away and I thought that was it.

Lynette Leave him. It's easier said than done, that's all. Looking at it from the outside, it's easy. But it's not easy from the inside. Thinking of going is just as terrible as staying. You don't know what will happen. It's the unknown. Being on your own.

Yes, I'm a coward. But then he says he's sorry, and he'll never do it again, and he won't drink so much. He's considerate and spends his time in the house doing jobs, and I can hear him about, and in the shed, hammering and sawing and whistling . . . there's something . . . and I know it won't last . . . and I know I'm a fool to pretend . . . but when it gets something like how I would like it to be between us, and I start to feel happy, it's like I start to put all the bad things away in a cupboard. And I know you think that's stupid but I can't help myself, because my mother taught me that a marriage is sacred and you should try your best to make it work for better or worse. I know what I should do. But I can't help the way I am. I can't change . . . not yet.

Ruby Then there was the go-kart. He was at the door again one afternoon. 'I've made this for Carl,' he said, and stood back and a little red painted cart was there on the path and some boys had followed it up the street and were looking from the gate, and then Carl was under my arm and seeing it. I told him Carl wouldn't take it, we didn't want anything from him, and he walked off. 'Take it with you, don't want it', I said, but he just went, and the boys at the gate looked as if to say, 'I'll have it'. And I would have given it to them but Carl was with me with the same look. I made him come in the house and closed the door.

At tea-time I found him at the front window, looking, and it was still there and still the boys were at the gate. Over tea I had to try to tell him why we couldn't take it, but I couldn't answer him when he asked me who the man was. I made him go out and lock it in the shed until we thought about it a bit more. He was happy and heartbroken at the same time and I couldn't look at him when he gave me the key back.

He's a good boy. I won't let that man come into his life.

Lynette We were all right again for a while. Really all right. But yes it started again and was worse and I found some courage and said I WAS leaving and going to my Dad's but even as I said it I knew that couldn't happen because Dad was getting married again and she wouldn't want me there, I had nowhere to go. 'And anyway,' Royce said, 'if you go, I'll find you' and he held my neck to show me what he meant.

Ruby Then there was the knife. I found it when I was emptying his school lunch box. (*To* **Carl**.) Where did this come from?

Carl I made a swap for something.

Ruby What? (*To us*.) But he couldn't think straight off.

Carl Some marbles.

Ruby (*to us*) And I knew he was lying to me. (*To him*.) What are you doing with this? Who gave you this? Tell me!

Carl That man.

Ruby What man? (*To us*.) Royce had been waiting outside school and walked along with him. (*To him.*) What have I told you about talking to strangers?

Carl He's not a stranger.

Ruby We don't know him. We don't want to know him.

Carl He's my Dad.

Ruby NO. Now listen! Listen to me Carl. Carl! . . . (*To us.*) And he ran out into the street. I put the knife in the dustbin.

I thought twice about Elaine's offer after that, and decided to let Carl go with them. They're back this week-end. I gave the go-kart away. But it came back again.

Jodie I did Royce's wife's hair the other day. I recognised her from that time I went in his shop. Her father was getting married again, she said. She wanted it doing for the wedding. Royce wasn't mentioned. We just talked about how the town has changed. She said about the lock-keeper's cottage. I used to wonder what it was like living there, sitting in my little hollow on the hill, watching the smoke rise from the chimney. And it had been her home. And now she was living over a shop, with him. She asked me round to see her photographs of the lock and the river – how it used to be . . . and I said yes, I would like that.

Ruby I gave the go-kart to Bernice up the street for her boy. I told her where it came from. He fell in love with it straight away. A couple of days later she brought it back and told me about the man in the park. I have to go round and get Royce to stop what he's doing to us.

During the following speech we gradually become aware that **Lynette** *is unable to move without considerable pain to her neck and back.*

Lynette My father was married yesterday. The wedding went well. We had the reception at the co-op. That was when he started. Drinking too much and talking too loud and starting to say things to me, showing me up in front of my family and my stepmother's family. The women look, and the men laugh and think he's a man's man, and he's buying drinks and telling dirty jokes and they laugh, and the women look, and I want to go before something happens, I'm so nervous.

In the end I left him to it, came away. I don't suppose you can understand, but I wanted to go to the cemetery to see my mother, have a little talk – not because of Dad marrying again, just . . . anyway, I didn't go. I didn't have the bus fare.

I came home and waited. When he finally came in I couldn't stop him. He was too strong. I wasn't going to go anywhere. I wasn't going to get away from him. I couldn't go anywhere. I couldn't leave. I couldn't move. (*Pause.*) And then, when he finished –

Royce *is heard approaching, whistling. It gets closer, into the room, stops.*

Royce, please. Don't hurt me again. (*Pause.*) What are you doing? (*She tries to turn round to see him, but can't.*) Royce, please, don't. Say something. Where are you? Don't do anything. I won't try to leave. I promise. (*Pause.*) Say something! (*The whistling begins again, moving off.*) Where are you going? Royce! Royce!

In pain, she manages to stand.

The taps come on, and run the water fast into the sink. (*She makes her way across to the dresser.*) And then the razor sloshing in the bowl, and he would be leaning into the mirror, wiping the steam away, concentrating . . .

She looks in a drawer, empties it. Feels the weight of the drawer in her hands.

I have to do it, I have to do it now.

She makes her way to the door as the light fades. The whistling stops in the dark. Suddenly the shop door bell rings loudly and a shaft of light comes up on **Jodie** *in the shop.*

Jodie I didn't expect the shop to be open on a Sunday morning. (*Pause.*) She might be at church. I was up this way anyway. (*Looks round.*) Royce Boland's. Selling guns and knives now as well as fishing tackle.

Lynette *appears.*

Hello. (*Pause.*) You said about the photographs. (*Pause.*) I did your hair.

Lynette Yes. (*Pause.*) Come on up.

They move off. The lights come up in the room.

Jodie Would it be better if I came another day?

Lynette No. I'm all right. It's a bit of back trouble I've been getting. Just takes me a bit longer to get about. Makes me so I can't concentrate sometimes, when it's bad.

Jodie Oh, dear.

They sit.

How did the wedding go?

Lynette It was lovely. They had a lovely day. (*Pause.*) The weather kept nice for them, didn't it?

Jodie It did, yes. How was your back yesterday?

Lynette Not too bad. It might have been all the dancing.

Jodie Yes.

Lynette It was a lovely day. We had the co-op.

Jodie Oh yes, it's nice there. My cousin had it for hers.

Lynette I've got to get used to having a mother again now.

Jodie Are they having a honeymoon?

Lynette Yes. Torquay.

Jodie Lovely.

Lynette I hope the weather keeps nice for them.

Jodie Yes. It's been a good summer, really, hasn't it?

Lynette Yes. (*Pause.*) Photographs.

She makes to get them, painfully.

Jodie Are you sure?

Lynette I'll get them. Now, where though?

Jodie Did you take any yesterday?

Lynette I haven't got a camera. I'll be able to choose from the proper pictures when they get them. Order some prints.

The shop door bell rings loudly again. A shaft of light comes up on **Ruby**.

I didn't put the catch on, did I? What do they want on a Sunday?

Jodie I'll go.

Lynette What?

Jodie I'd better go.

Lynette No, I can see to it.

Jodie No, I mean I'd better leave.

Lynette No, you stay.

Jodie Let me tell them to go, then, unless it's important. You sit down. You can't keep going up and down stairs.

Jodie *goes out.* **Lynette** *sits.*

Ruby (*to us*) I've practised this speech. Started learning it in bed last night. The little cart is in the boot of my car. I can't bring it straight in, in case his wife is about.

Lynette *suddenly freezes in fear as the sound of running water is heard.*

Lynette (*to herself*) The water. It's running again. It's running again.

Jodie *appears with* **Ruby**.

Jodie Yes?

Ruby Hello. I was just wondering if Mr Boland was in?

Jodie No, sorry.

Lynette (*to herself*) Royce.

Ruby Do you know when he'll be back?

Jodie No. Can I give a message to his wife to pass on?

Lynette (*petrified as she begins to understand*) Royce.

Ruby No, it'll wait.

Lynette NO!

Jodie *and* **Ruby** *run in. The sound of water stops.*

Listen. The water. It's stopped. The water –

The three of them turn suddenly to the doorway.

Don't let him hurt me again. Royce I'm sorry. I didn't mean it. Don't let him hurt me again. (*Backing off.*) I'm sorry . . . Oh God, help me. (*To us.*) HELP ME!

Blackout.

The three women are stood together.

Ruby (*to us*) If anybody asks, I went to see Royce Boland about taking back the cart. The shop was open . . . but there was no-one in. I left. I drove home. At one o'clock I went to the railway station and met my sister Elaine and her husband and their daughter Sandra, and my son Carl, and I brought them home.

Jodie If anybody asks, I went to see Lynette Boland to see some photographs. She showed me them. Her husband was not there. I left about half past twelve. I went home, had my dinner. Tim came round and we went for a walk . . . along the river. We walked back. I went in, had my tea, watched television, had a bath.

The two women take **Lynette**'*s hands in theirs to help her.*

Lynette I couldn't do it by myself. (**Jodie** *and* **Ruby** *try to pull away but she holds them both close, and carries on.*) One of them had a car. She brought it round the back. The other one got something to cover him with from the shed. We couldn't move him from the bottom of the stairs. She had a little red cart. We got him on it, pulled him out of the house with the sheet over and lifted him into the back of the car. I went in and did a bit of cleaning. They drove him to the quarry. To make him look like he had fallen, you see . . . as if he has fallen over the top.

If anybody asks, he went for a walk on his own after dinner. Said he was going up the river. He was a bit depressed. We've not been getting on. It wasn't working out. I told him I was leaving . . . It was finished.

Pond Life

Characters

Trevor Buckfield, *twenty-three, shy*
David Buckfield, *twelve or thirteen, step-brother to Trevor*
Cassie Buckfield, *David's sister, about fifteen or sixteen*
Malcolm Panks, *sixteen, just left school, works for the Parks Department on a YTS scheme, loves space invaders and Cassie*
Shane, *best friend of Dave, about twelve*
Pogo, *a girl of eighteen, mentally ill*
Maurice Edlington, *seventeen or eighteen, a bit of a thug, Cassie's boyfriend*

Scenario

Midsummer, Stainforth, a village in South Yorkshire. Trevor, unemployed, spends his days fishing, making floats in his shed, or helping his friend Pogo, who is mentally ill, by making cassette tapes for her. When Trevor's step brother Dave and his friend Shane see a giant carp almost caught in the local ponds, Trevor organizes a Saturday night carp fishing expedition for them all. It turns out to be a summer night none of them will forget.

Pond Life was first performed at the Bush Theatre on 5 June 1992 in association with the Royal National Theatre Studio with the following cast:

Dave	Lyndon Davies
Maurice	Joe Duttine
Malcolm	James Hooton
Shane	Paul McCready
Cassie	Isobel Raine
Pogo	Joanna Robinson
Trevor	Richard Standing

Directed by Simon Usher
Designed by Anthony Lambe
Lighting by Sam Moon
Sound by Paul Bull

Fade up interior, shed. **Trevor** *is sorting through a fishing tackle box. He begins sandpapering a float. A little movement.*

Pogo Sssh. Listen.

A portable tape recorder clicks on to play. We hear a recording of exterior, quiet street, with **Pogo** *speaking into the microphone of the recorder. Sandpapering stops.*

'One, two, three, testing. One – One – My dad got me another blank cassette so I'm making a summer special. (*She makes the sound of an Hawaiian guitar playing the* Third Man *theme.*) Saturday morning, South Pacific. No, it isn't really, it's Stainforth, but it is quite sunny. I'm in our street. There's a pit up that way but you can't see it 'cos it's round the corner, and that way down there is where my grandma used to live. It's going to be hot, like yesterday. There was all tar melting in our back street, yesterday, I was poking it. (*Pause.*) I don't know what to say now. (*Pause.*) There's a dog over there.'

The tape runs on. Blank. A click on the tape. It runs on.

Pogo Wait, there's another bit in a minute.

Another click on the tape.

'The bread van's stopped at Mrs Poppleton's shop and he's taking the tray in. There's a woman coming up the street now. I'm off to say something.'

Sound of footsteps approaching on the tape.

'Hello.'

'Hello, love.'

'It's nice, isn't it?'

'Yes, it's lovely, love. It wants to stop like it now for a bit.'

'Yes.'

Footsteps recede.

'She didn't know I was recording. There's David over there. His brother is my best friend.'

(*Calling.*) 'Hello, David.'

(*From across the street.*) 'Hello, Pogo.'

'Is your Trevor in?'

'He's in his shed.'

(**Pogo**, *close to microphone.*) 'I'm off to see Trev in his shed now, so Roger over and out.'

The recording clicks off, followed by the tape recorder being switched off in the shed.

Pogo   That's it, Trev.

Trev   That's good.

Pogo   That was your David.

Trev   I know.

Pogo   Can I do you now?

Trev   Let me think of something good to say first. Don't waste your tape.

Gentle sandpapering begins again.

Pogo   This is going to be my best summer. I'd like to tape it all. Stop it going away. (*Pause.*) Things do, though, don't they? Even real important things go. They start to break up and float away and you can't reach them. Instead you get things stuck in your head that you don't want. (*Pause.*) Yasser Arrafat and that. (*Pause.*) I haven't any stories from when I was little to tell my children. I won't be having any children. I'm a woman, aren't I Trev? (*Pause.*) Little bits of memories float about in my head like snow in one of them glass ball snowstorms. Only it never settles. I'm gone in the head, aren't I, Trev?

Trev   No.

Pogo   What would I do without you?

Trev   You're not what you said.

Pogo   No? I'm harmless. I'm that little fat barmy lass that Trevor Buckfield looks after. You're saddled with me, you know.

Sandpapering stops. He blows on the float.

Trev There. Another float finished. Just wants some varnish now.

Pogo Taking me fishing when you want to be on your own.

Trev I think I'll put some stronger line on that reel you're using.

Pogo Out of the house at half past eight Saturday morning, waiting for Trev to get up. Chucking pebbles at his window. As soon as he's in his shed, Pogo's at the door. 'Oooh, Trev, are you there?'

Trev I thought you wanted to come with me. You said you did last night.

Pogo I do, Trev, I do.

Trev It'll be great, won't it, if we catch her.

Pogo Will it be something I won't forget?

Trev Oh, when that line goes out and the reel starts screaming . . . it's magic. It's something really special catching your first carp.

Pogo Oh, Trev, it would be great, wouldn't it? I really would like to catch a big fish like that.

Trev Yes, so would I.

Pogo If she's a monster she wants a name. Nessie. I'm off to call her Nessie. Like Moby Dick. What if she pulls me in? Drags me round the pond all tangled in fishing line? Coming up for air. 'Thar she blows!' That would be quite disastrous, wouldn't it? She won't get hurt. I want to catch her fair. Then we'll put her back. She won't die. She'll swim away and grow old and wise and no one will ever catch her for a hundred years. (*Pause – remembering.*) I had a goldfish. I used to have a goldfish. She died. I put her in a big match box and polyfilled it under my bedroom window sill, closer to heaven. In another house. When I lived somewhere else. There were daisies in the matchbox, I laid her in daisies. (*Pause.*) Who's seen her?

Trev   Our David's mate, Shane. Last night.

Pogo   I know that.

Trev   I've seen her.

Pogo   Tell me.

Trev   You remember.

Pogo   No, tell me again.

Trev   What colour is she?

Pogo   Golders Green.

Trev   What did she look like?

Pogo   A yellow submarine.

Trev   Where was she?

Pogo   Tell me.

Trev   She was under the broken –

Trev
Pogo } Willow tree.

Pogo   Yes.

Trev   Lying with the sun on her back.

Pogo   Yes.

Trev   Then she sensed me and slid slowly away, down into the deep water.

Pogo   Not a ripple, was there, Trev? Not even a little ripple, you said.

Trev   That's right. You remember, see?

Pogo   I remember. I want to see her. Will tonight be a good night?

Trev   I don't know. Some of the best times are heavy rain and thunderstorms. I've sat at night in thunderstorms and it's brought the fish on to feed like mad. I've had a net full by the time the storm has died away.

Pogo I feel it will be right. It has to be tonight. She'll be there, patrolling along the edge of the reeds, and I'll be there, waiting.

Trev In the right place at the right time, with the right tackle.

Pogo The right feeling. Like my mam some weeks at bingo. She knows she can't lose. Lucky night, lucky table, lucky pencil.

Trev Lucky floats. No. Not lucky. Just good to have around. Old friends. Delicate little floats. I look at them sometimes and I can see all the days we've had, sunrises and sunsets on the water. Precious. I can remember the first float my dad gave me. I was about ten. One shift he came home from the pit, didn't come in the house, came straight in here, picked up his rod and tackle bag and went out again. Not a word. Hours later my mam sent me down to the pond to fetch him home. I found him hunched over the rod, the little orange float out on the water in the darkness. There'd been an accident. One of his pals. He couldn't get to him. I didn't know what to say so I said supper was on the table. When he reeled in and lifted the rod there was no hook on the line, no bait. He'd been sat watching a float that was never going to move. I never said anything. I've still got that float. I never use it but it's always in my box. It's not there for catching fish.

Pogo That's not a made-up story, is it? (*Pause.*) Sometimes, I think I'd like to marry you.

Trev What you doing this afternoon?

Pogo Nothing. Why?

Trev You can help me mix all the baits and get the tackle ready.

Pogo Oh! (*Pause.*) Fat maggots in treacle.

From inside the shed we hear **Malcolm** *walking up the back alley,*

*whistling to himself. The sneck on the back gate is lifted. Back gate opens
and closes. He walks up the yard and into the shed.*

Malc   I've brought your mum's calamine lotion back, Trev.

Pogo   Hello, Malcolm.

Malc   Pogo.

Trev   Hello, Malc. She's in the back kitchen.

Malc   Oh. What you doing?

Trev   Nothing much. You been doing anything?

Malc   No. (*Pause.*) Is your Cassie in, Trev?

Trev   I think she's still in bed.

Pogo   What did you want her for?

Malc   Nowt.

Pogo   I thought she'd finished with you?

Malc   Get lost.

Trev   What's up, Malc?

Malc *takes a folded letter from his jeans.*

Malc   Will you give her this letter for me, Trev?

Pogo   I did get lost once.

Trev   She won't read it.

Pogo   I lost my mum in C and A's and I couldn't find my
way out.

Malc   OK.

He returns the letter to his pocket.

Pogo   We passed each other on the escalators.

*From inside the shed we can hear kids playing in the back alley – running,
bikes – into the distance.*

Trev   Why don't you come with us tonight?

Malc   Where?

Trev   We're off up Decoy Ponds after carp. Somebody nearly caught a massive one last night. It nearly pulled him in. Snapped twelve pound breaking strain line.

Malc   Who?

Trev   Some fella. Our kid's mate, Shane, was up there watching. Half an hour he had it on and then it snapped him.

Pogo   Twang. 'Bugger it', I bet he said. I would. My mam says I can go with Trevor so we're off. Their David's coming as well.

Malc   I'm off up the Golden Nuggett.

Pogo   Can I put one of your tapes on, Trev?

Trev   Sure. Well, you can come if you want, Malc.

Malc   I've got to get my old form back. I couldn't get anywhere near my best score on that Star Battler last night.

Pogo *is rummaging through cassette tapes.*

Trev   You were OK, then, after your mum put the calamine on?

Malc   Yes. It stopped stinging.

Pogo   What did you do?

She fits a cassette tape into deck.

Malc   Maurice Edlington threw me in some nettles. I only had my shorts on, 'cos it was hot.

Pogo   I know. There was all tar melting in our back street. I was poking it. Why did he throw you in the nettles?

Malc   Because he said I was looking at him.

Click. Fast forward on tape recorder.

Pogo   Why do you let your Cassie go out with him, Trev?

Trev   I don't. How's the job going, Malc?

Pogo   You do.

She presses stop button on tape.

Malc   It's all right. I bunked off on Thursday afternoon.

Pogo *presses play button. We hear* **Trevor**'s 'band' playing an early seventies number, recorded in the shed. It isn't very good. **Trev** turns it down. We hear **Pogo** over –

Pogo   I like tape recorders, do you, Malcolm? I've got loads of tapes. Top of the Pops; Top Forty; my mam talking to the budgie when she didn't know it was running; laughing and swearing at my dad; telly adverts; Trevor; I've got loads. It would all go away, you see, without the tapes. Like the budgie. She's gone now but I've got her on tape. She had a growth under her chin like a bit of brain so dad had to put her in a plastic bag and hold her over the gas ring. But I've still got the sound of her when she was chirping and bashing her bell to bits.

The song ends and straight away we cut into an even older number. **Trev** *on accoustic guitar sung to the tune of* 'One night with you' (*Elvis*).

Oh, oh, Maureen
You are a (*Pause whilst he finds the chord.*) dream.
I hope we never part
'Cos in my heart you're
(*Pause whilst he finds the chord.*) queen

Trev   Turn it off.

Pogo   What is it? No, leave it. Is that you? Who's Maureen?

Trev *clicks tape off, then presses fast forward.*

Spoilsport.

Trev   It was a girl I used to go out with.

Pogo   How long ago?

Trev   I were nowt but a young lad.

Malc   Have you heard them horror sound-effects tapes with torture on and stuff? A kid used to bring them to school and we used to listen to them in music. Some of it's dead good but some of it's crap. There's one that's supposed to be a bloke having his head chopped off. All they do is chop a cabbage in half. You can tell that's all it is. You could do it yourself.

On the tape we hear a new number by **Trev**'s *band. Softer.*

Pogo   Hey, how could you put a goldfish on tape? You couldn't do it, could you? (*Pause.*) Unless it was a dolphin. (*Makes dolphin noises.*)

Malc   That's a bloody peacock, int it? Here then, here, have a fish and shut it.

Pogo (*stopping dolphin impression*)   Mmm, fish food. Hey, we're doing fish food this afternoon, aren't we, Trev? There's your Cassie coming down the yard, Trev.

Cassie *enters shed.*

Cassie   Will you take me to the shop on your bike?

Trev   No.

Cassie   Why not?

Trev   I'm busy.

Malc   I'll go for you.

Cassie   No thanks.

Cassie *leaves.* **Malc** *jumps up and follows. Exterior, the yard.*

Malc (*calling*)   Cassie.

Cassie   What?

Malc (*closer*)   I – er – I wanted to talk to you.

Cassie   I don't talk to puffs.

We hear footsteps recede, the back gate opened and closed. We can still just hear the music tape. **Malc** *goes back in shed.*

Pogo   What did she say?

Malc   She says she wants time to think about it.

The music fades.

Fade in exterior. A small wood near open fields. Sound of two boys running down a hill towards us. Laughing, making their voices shake as they run and tumble. They come into the wood.

Dave   I'm a grizzly, right, and you're a trapper.

They climb a tree, feet on branches, swaying.

Shane   You can't get me up here.

Dave   Yea I can, bears can climb trees.

Shane   I stab you with a knife.

Dave   You ant got a knife.

Shane   Yea I have.

Dave   All right, then, I shake the tree and make you drop it.

Shane   Yea, but it falls on your head and digs into your brain.

Dave   Yea, but not enough to kill me. It just digs in a bit and that sends me berserk and I grab your leg with my claws. Aaaaargggh. Ggrrrr.

The branches sway more violently.

Shane   Oh, get off. Get off, Dave! That hurts. Get off you dirty sod you've slavered all over my leg.

Shane *jumps down from the tree.*

Dave   Sos. Sos, Shane.

Shane   Get lost.

Pause. They pull stems of grass to chew.

Dave   Let's go and see if there are any courting couples to watch.

Shane   No, I don't want to.

Dave   My cousin says there's loads on Hexthorpe Flatts near where he lives. You're stepping over them wherever you go, he says. Like dog muck.

Dave *spits out a bit of chewed grass.*

Shane   I'm not in the mood. I went last night.

Dave   See owt?

Shane   No.

Dave   We could get in the mood.

Shane   No, I just don't feel like it today.

Dave   Let's put the bits of that centre page together, eh? I'll get the tin out of the den.

Dave *moves through trees to the den, a little way off.*

Shane (*calling*)   Why do we have to wait till tonight to catch that fish?

Dave (*from in the den*)   I've told you, it's too hot. Trev says they don't feed much during the day.

Dave *returns, opens tin.*

We should have put numbers on the back of these bits.

Shane   Is this her arm?

Dave   No, her leg.

Shane   You should have stuck her down on a piece of card.

Dave   Yea, but I like fitting all the bits together. I can save the best bits till last.

Shane   Hey, that polaroid photo that Grout brought to school of his sister.

Dave   He thought it was great, didn't he?

Shane   He thought we'd all be going pop-eyed.

They laugh.

Dave   Lisa Grout in her bra and pants!

They laugh again. Louder, beginning to get silly.

Shane   You could only tell it was female because of the bra!

Dave   Maybe it was him in her undies!

Shane   Maybe it was the dog!

They are falling about, hysterical.

Dave   Hey, do you know where it is now?

Shane   No, where?

Dave   He got it confiscated in 'Learning for Living'.

Shane   I bet Dicko's got it pinned up in his stock room.

Dave   I bet he gave him the money to buy another film.

Pause. Their laughter subsides.

Shane   I wouldn't mind a polaroid.

Dave   You haven't got a sister.

Shane   Eh? No, I mean taking decent photos.

Dave   Yea. Hey, that couple we saw when we thought she had a bandage on her knee but it was her knickers.

Shane   No, I mean proper photos, like sunsets and that, and street lights, and snow. Like tonight. I could take a photo of us down at the ponds, and that big carp after I've caught it, so I've got proof.

Dave   After you've fallen in.

Shane   Or one of us all sat round a fire.

Dave   Our Trev's got some photos of him. One with three big tench and one with a keep net full of roach.

Shane   You know what they are, all the different fish?

Dave   Some of them.

Shane   You don't go fishing with your Trev much, though, do you?

Dave   No. I've been a couple of times. It's all right. I like sea fishing. We used to have a photo of me and Cassie and my dad on a boat in Whitby harbour with loads of cod.

Shane   Your real dad?

Dave   Yes.

Shane   I wouldn't mind going sea fishing. Shark fishing. I bet it was great living up near there, wasn't it?

Dave   Yea. I think my mum would like us all to move back if my dad wasn't living there. I don't think we will, though.

Shane   If you did I could come and visit you.

Dave   Yea.

Shane   I'm glad you came down here to live. (*Pause.*) Your Trev wouldn't want to move up there, would he?

Dave   No. He wouldn't mind us moving though, and him staying

Shane   Why's that?

Dave   There's not much room. And like, he's my step-brother and that but he's twenty-three and he feels a bit out of place with me and Cassie. We're not really interested much in each other. I wouldn't mind getting to know him a bit, but he's a bit old. He doesn't do anything.

Shane   He used to have a rock band.

Dave   I know, I've heard some of their tapes.

Shane   Him and Vic and Maurice Edlington and a couple of others. We all thought they were great. They were a right bunch of fucking weirdos but all us little kids used to go mad on them. He'd open his shed door so we could listen and we'd all do head banging in the back street.

Dave   He makes tapes for Pogo now.

Shane   Does he? What for?

Dave   She likes to listen.

Shane   My dad says she'll never make eighteen.

Dave   She is eighteen.

Shane   Christ.

Dave   She proved him wrong, then, dint she?

Shane   Yea. (*Pause.*) I don't know what to say now.

Dave   Say, 'I'm an idiot'.

Shane   You're an idiot.

Dave (*in a Dalek type voice*)   This conversation will self-destruct in five seconds. One.

Shane   I'm rewinding. Blurbulurbulurb.

Dave   Two.

Shane   It's gone.

Dave   Three.

Shane   I've erased it.

Dave   Quick. Open your mouth, open your mouth! (**Dave** *takes out* **Shane**'s *'words' and throws them like a hand grenade.*) Give it
me. Right. Get down. Neeeaaah Patoom!

Shane   Hey, throw a hand grenade in that pond tonight. We'd catch that fish then, wouldn't we?

Dave   Eh, yea, and every other fish. They'd all be floating on the top.

Shane   Eh, throw a hand grenade down one of them mole holes in that field. Little blind mole rooting and sniffing about. Patoom!

Dave   Them Vietking, I mean Vietcong, in them underground dens. Patoom! Hey, I'm Rambo, right, and you're a Vietcong.

Shane   Oh, it's always me.

Dave   No. You were Rambo when we were at the allotments.

Shane   All right. You're walking along the path, right, and

I'm hiding. I jump out and chop you with my fechete.

Shane *runs on ahead.*

Dave (*calling*)   Machete.

Shane (*distant*)   OK. Machete.

Dave   Fechete. Sounds like somebody in the mafia.

He machine guns **Shane**.

Shane (*distant*)   I'm not ready yet!

Machine gun fire. Calls of 'you're dead', etc. As the two boys run through the wood, voices echoing, receding.

Fade in interior, the shed. Another number is playing on the tape recorder, **Pogo** *sings along to it. It finishes.*

Pogo   We've got a majorette's uniform at our house. Everybody says it's what I used to wear. But it isn't.

Malc   Trev?

Trev   Mmm?

Malc   How long did it take you to get over that Maureen?

Trev   A few months.

Malc   Can't you stop Cassie going out with Maurice Edlington?

Trev   For you?

Malc   For hersen. He's turning her against everybody. Can't you see that?

Trev   It's not really for me to tell her, is it?

Malc   Do you hate him?

Trev   No.

Malc   His brother Vic was your best mate, wasn't he? They used to be a couple of good kids, him and Maurice. Before.

Pogo   Cassie had a nail and she scratched his name on her arm and made it bleed and then she rubbed some muck on it.

I told her but you can't tell them anything. Did I do things like that? I've had some needles in my arm.

Trev   There's nothing you can do, Malc.

Malc   I can't stop thinking about her, though. I'm up the YTS, cutting grass, taking up dead plants, kneeling down, and I'm like praying she's going to come by. I can't do the job properly. I put some plants in one morning and took them all out again in the afternoon. I can't do anything. I can't even get a decent score any more.

Trev   You can't make somebody like you.

Malc   At night, I sometimes try to astral project myself into her bedroom – I don't mean – I don't mean to do anything. I mean just to be there putting my thoughts inside her head. (*Pause.*) I feel so bad about her sometimes I just want to disappear inside myself. Especially when there are other people around. You know what I mean? Sometimes I think I'd like to get inside one of them video games, like in that film, only never come out again. Don't say owt, will you, Trev?

Trev   No.

Malc   Pogo?

Pogo   If I was a majorette, why haven't I got a bugle? I've got a sailor's cap but that doesn't mean I was in the navy. And a Davy Crockett hat.

Malc   I think I'll get off.

Trev   OK, see you.

Pogo   Malcolm?

Malc   What?

Pogo   It would be nice if you could come with us tonight. Really.

Malc   Thanks. I might see you, then. (*He leaves.*)

Pogo   I know what he means. Hiding inside a game. When it feels so bad but you don't want people to see. You wish you were invisible. My mum gets like that about me. My dad gets like that about my mum. (*Pause.*) I'm on the floor and I wake up and my mum is sat by me, next to the sofa, fitting a jigsaw together, and a tear drops into the box and I know I must have just had another fit.

Pause. **Trev** *picks up his accoustic guitar, strums.*

Trev I was going to do you a tape.

Pogo What for? It's not time for me to go away again.

Trev I just wanted to do you one.

Pogo Like my summer special? You can do it on mine.

Trev I think I want to do it separate.

Pogo Will you do me a love song? So I can remember Malcolm in love in my summer. Will you do me one on your guitar?

Trev I'll have a go.

We hear gentle strumming, picking, nothing in particular.

Pogo Is that it?

Trev I'm thinking.

Pogo I'll think too, shall I? (*Pause. Just guitar.*) I can't think when I'm hungry. Is it dinner time?

Trev Not far off.

Pogo I'm off home, then, I think, Trev. I'll see you later.

Trev Yea. See you.

Pogo *leaves.* **Trev** *continues playing the guitar for a while then thinks of a song, possibly 'Bridge Over Troubled Water' which he plays and sings a few bars of. Stops. Puts a tape into recorder. Presses record. Clears his throat.*

One. One.

A few bars of 'Bridge' then a wrong chord. Stops.

I'll work the song out later. I'll just put this bit on now. (*Pause.*)

I can't get a flat in Stainforth, you see, and there's not really much room at home now. I'm getting under people's feet a bit. That's why I'm always in here, I suppose. So . . . I'm moving. Only to Doncaster. My Aunty Betty in Hexthorpe works in Pennywise and she says there might be a job coming up. Just in the warehouse, moving boxes. I've got a flat fixed up near the hospital on Armthorpe Road. I've seen about the dole and that. It's not a bad little flat. Course, I won't be able to take all my tackle so I'll leave you in charge. I've told my dad to let you come in the shed if you want. (*Pause.*) I'll miss you. I can't stay here, though, can I? Not for ever. I can't take you with me.

Click. Rewind. Playback.

'I've told my dad to let you come in the shed if you want.'

Click. Record again.

You look after things here. I'll come and see you. I'll do you some tapes. You look after your mum and dad and Trevor's shed. Look after all the gear for when I come over and we go on some more fishing expeditions. Think about those weekends down at Decoy Ponds, eh? Love you.

Click. Silence.

Wasteland. **Malcolm** *is lying spread-eagled on his belly with his coat wrapped tightly around his head.*

Malc   It's me, Malcolm Panks. I'm not anybody. You've got me mixed up with someone else. Honest. Look, I can't keep still any longer. My rash. It's itching. Listen. Please listen to me. Just let me scratch. Don't drop the boulder on my head. (*Pause.*) Look, what do you want?

Dave *and* **Shane** *enter, they sit and watch.*

Malc   I've told you. I don't go out with Cassie Buckfield. Are you there? Who are you? What do you want? Look, I'm Malcolm Panks, you've got the wrong person. Let me show you. Right? Don't drop the boulder, I'm just going to show you, right? I'm getting neck ache for Christ's sake! I used to go out with her – yea, OK – I used to but I finished with her. I don't see her now. Is it because of that? Look, if it's about that plastic stork I pinched, I didn't know it was your garden. Is it that? I'm suffocating.

Dave   Hey Panksy, what's up?

Shane   What are you talking to yourself for?

They help him unravel his coat and sit him up.

Shane   Who were you talking to?

Malcolm *looks round, gasping for air.*

Malc   Where've they gone?

Dave   Who?

Malc   Them kids.

Dave   What did they do?

Malc   Nearly killed me. Crazy. They nearly did.

Shane   Let's go after them.

Dave   Yea, come on.

Malc   No, no don't. They're nutters. Leave it. One of them was massive.

Dave   Yea? You see them?

Malc   I was just laid down here, playing with my space invader, and I put my coat over my head to keep the sun out. Next thing they were on top of me. One of them had steel caps, I think.

Shane   Skinheads.

Malc   Yea, a bunch of skins. I think they could have been mates of Maurice Edlington. He could have been with them but he let the others do the talking.

Dave   What did they say?

Malc   One of them just said, 'We've got a brick here and we're gonna cave your head in if you move.'

Shane   Hey, there were some kids in the chip shop on about getting a kid.

Dave   Yea, skinheads.

Malc   That's 'em.

Dave   What you going to do?

Malc (*getting up*)   I'm off home. I keep getting smacked in every time I come out. (*He goes.*)

Dave and **Shane** *fall about laughing.*

Dave   Hey, do you like my steelies?

Shane   'Oh, you're sitting on my nettle rash.'

Dave   I like your skinhead haircut.

They go off. **Cassie** *and* **Maurice** *appear.*

Maurice   I'm thinking of having my hair cut.

Cassie   I'll do it for you.

Maurice   I might go into Donny, have it red round here.

Cassie   It'll look nice.

Maurice   My mam says I'll look like a carbuncle.

Cassie   A what?

Pause. They sit. **Cassie** *begins writing her name on* **Maurice**'s *arm in biro.*

Cassie   What are we doing tonight, then? There's nothing to do round here, is there? It was better where I was. At least there was somewhere to go. I hate this place. Have you ever thought of leaving?

Maurice   I never stop thinking of it.

Cassie   Why haven't you?

Maurice   My dad and my brother's gone. I don't want my mam to be left on her own.

Cassie   Why, is she old?

Maurice   No, she just looks it.

Pause.

Cassie   We could get some cider from the beer off and go on the school field tonight.

Maurice   No.

Cassie   I could ring Arlene up and see if we can watch their video. Her mum and dad go out on a Saturday night up the welfare.

Maurice   What they got?

Cassie   They had 'Death Wish Two' last week.

Pause.

Maurice   Did you hear about them two kids in Rossington? Their parents didn't want them to go together and his family were leaving town. D'you know what they did?

Cassie   Yea, I know.

Maurice   They stood between the rails, hand in hand, in front of the Scunthorpe train. (*Pause.*) I could do that. Giz a job. I could do that. Maybe I could do it for you.

Cassie   Maurice.

Maurice   Cassie. I was lying.

Cassie   You get me all confused.

Maurice   That makes two of us.

Cassie   I can't work you out. (*Pause.*) I'm sorry. I just want to get to know you, that's all. You never tell me anything about yourself.

Maurice   You want to ask around a bit, then.

Cassie   I don't listen to what other people say.

Pause. They get serious.

Maurice   Huh.

Cassie   What?

Maurice   I was just thinking – if you don't listen to gossip and I never tell you anything, we could last a fair bit.

Cassie   If you want us to.

Maurice   Do you?

Cassie   Do you? What's wrong?

Maurice   You never give me a straight answer.

Cassie   I do.

Maurice   Do you want us to finish?

Cassie   If you want us to.

Maurice   See? You don't mind if we finish, then?

Cassie   I never said that.

Maurice   Why can't you tell me what you think?

Cassie   I'm scared to.

Maurice   Why?

Cassie   Because – I'm scared that if you really know what I think about you, you'll get scared and leave me.

Maurice   I don't scare easy. (*Mocking.*) I'm hard me, I'm steel.

Cassie   Yea?

Maurice *squashes coke can.*

Maurice   One hand.

Cassie   Yea, well I'm still not telling you.

They mess about, a little mock fight.

Ah, I'm falling back. Don't! Ah! Maurice!

(*Laughter.*)

Pull me up, then.

Maurice   You don't spell it like that, do you?

Cassie   What?

Maurice   Cassie – that on your arm.

Cassie   Yes.

Maurice   I've spelt it with a K.

Cassie   Where?

Maurice   I tattooed it on my leg.

Cassie   You daft get. Let's have a look.

Maurice   Get off! Not in the street, give over.

Laughing, **Cassie** *chases* **Maurice** *along the street.*

Fade in, interior, the shed. **Pogo** *is coming down the yard from* **Trev***'s back door, singing to herself.*

Pogo   Half a pound of tuppeny rice
Half a pound of treacle
Mix them up and make them nice
Pop goes the weazle

She comes into the shed and begins mixing the fish bait.

A stir for luck, a spit for luck. (*Spits in bowl.*) Hubble bubble toil and trouble. Pint of maggots, jar of worms, cat food, dog food, fish food, elephant's poop, bull's blood. Mix me a match, catch me a catch. Walk three times backwards round it and then you'll see the fish you're going to marry.

Alone in the shed, **Pogo***'s inner voices and fragments of memories begin to stir . . .*

Pogo   Round and round
down and down
                              Like a whirlpool
I'm going to be at
Decoy Ponds, fishing.
                              Drowning.
That old black magic has me
in its spell.

Dragging you down

I'm going to catch a
big fish.

Drowning

Get out! Bugger off!
You have to spoil it,
don't you. Nasty voices.
Keep away!

(*She hums the tune of 'Half a Pound . . .' then sings, to same tune . . .*)

I'm not going to let you in
I'm thinking of something else.
Fish and chips and Trevor and me,
Off fishing this evening.

(*Frightened.*) Trevor, hurry up and come back with the stuff. I
don't want to be on my own.

(*Singing.*) I won't let the sun go down on me I won't let the sun
go down.

(*Getting distressed.*) 'There's nothing you can't do if you put your
mind to it', as my old grandad used to say.

Did he?

I don't know, I never had a grandad, I was making it up.

Aye, well, there's nowt so queer as folk, is there?

You're bloody queer. You're mental.

'If tha ever does owt for nowt, allus do it for thysen.'

(*Singing through tears.*) There's nothing you can do
that can't be done
There's nothing you can sing that can't be sung.
There's nothing you can say
But you can learn how to play the game
it's easy
All you need is love . . .

You're mental. You're barmy. (*Singing.*) Pogo is a nut case,
you're a fruit and nut case.

Your brain's dissolving. It's turning to slush. Your head's a
slush puppy machine.
I don't want you. You're not getting in. I won't let you get in.
I'm thinking of . . . I'm thinking of . . .

(*Singing.*) The most beautiful drink in the world
That's Martini.
Any time any place any where . . .

You wet the bed.

Don't tell anybody. Please don't tell anybody.

You piss yourself. You can't even control your own bladder.

(*Very fast.*) I'm trying. I'm trying to be . . . I'm trying to keep
afloat. Floats. Delicate little floats. Precious. It's always in my
box. It's not there for catching fish.

It's the glorious sixteenth today, Pogo, let's go down to the lake
and fish for tench. We'll try the lift method. It's deadly for
bottom feeders like the noble tench. You put a worm on and
I'll try bread.

Look, my float's moving!

Wait. Strike!

It's on. Wow! It's going like a train.

Looks like worm is the bait today.

Oh, Trevor, I'm losing it. Hurry up. I'm losing my thoughts.
It's going to snap the line. It's getting away.

'Stopping By Woods On A Snowy Evening' by Robert Frost.

Whose woods these are I think –

I want to throw up, talking about poems, you fat pig.

The woods are lovely, dark and deep,
But I have promises to keep
And miles to go before I sleep
And miles to go before –

I put you to sleep like a pig shot with a bolt through the head.

Putting the wrong words into my head. Making me think bad words. Please make them stop, Jesus.

Jesus is a –

No! Don't make me think that about him. Don't make me say that. I love you, Jesus.

(*Singing.*) I love thee lord Jesus
        I ask thee to stay
        Close by me for ever
        And love me I pray.

        Jesus is a –

Puts her hand over her mouth, then her fingers in her mouth to try and stop the words coming out.

Jesus is a – Mmmmmm

Wash your mouth out with soap and water!

Pogo *begins to fill her mouth with the fish food mix. Coughing, baulking.* **Trev** *runs in, drops tackle.* **Pogo** *is crying and coughing.*

Trev   It's all right. It's all right. I'm here. You're all right. You're not supposed to eat it. It's bait for the carp, fish bait. (*Pause.*) Let me get a cloth. (*Comforting her, but a little embarrassed.*) That's a good mix. You've mixed that well. It's got to be the right consistency, hasn't it? Not too soft or it would come off the hook when you cast out. Not too hard or when the fish picks it up and you strike, the hook won't pull through onto his lip. This is about right. We'll put this in the bait boxes. You fill this one, eh? (*He begins to transfer the mixture from bowl to plastic bait box.*) I got this recipe out of 'Angler's Mail'. They did a thing all about special baits for carp in last week's. High protein. You can catch them on most things, though. If they're used to finding it. Banana, even.

Pogo *starts to lose control again, sobs.*

It's all right, I'm here.

We hear running up the yard from the house. **Dave** *dives into the shed.*

Dave   Hi, Trev. We've come to help you get all the tackle ready. My mam's doing the sandwiches. She wants to know do we want tea or coffee in the flask.

Trev   Coffee.

Dave (*going out*)   Right. (*To* **Shane**, *who is stood outside.*) It's all right, you're allowed in.

Shane *steps in.* **Dave** *goes back up yard.*

Trev   Hello, Shane.

Shane   I'm borrowing a rod. My mam's getting it this afternoon.

Trev   What sort?

Shane   A fishing rod.

Trev   Yea, I know, but what type?

Dave (*from up the yard*)   Coffee! Mam, coffee! (*Runs back.*)

Trev   Is it a float rod, carp rod, pike rod, leger rod?

Shane   My uncle bought it at Bridlington.

Dave *steps in.*

Dave   What?

Shane   That rod I'm getting.

Trev   A sea fishing rod?

Shane   Yes.

Trev   You can't – Oh, it'll do.

Dave   How long are we staying out?

Shane   Will we need sleeping bags?

Dave   It gets cold at night, dunt it, Trev? I'm wearing a pair of my mam's old – tights.

Shane   You puff.

Dave   They keep your legs warm, don't they, Trev?

Shane   Do you wear women's tights, Trev?

Trev   Sometimes.

Pause.

Shane   What's it like?

Trev   It's all right. Look, you two can be putting the rods and the bank sticks into my holdall.

Dave   I wish we could stay out all night.

Trev   Well you can't.

Dave   In the morning, walking home with all your catch.

The boys begin to sort tackle.

Trev   If you catch anything you put it straight back.

Dave   Get stuffed. I'm keeping it. If I catch it, I keep it.

Trev   No. Any fish caught go back unharmed.

Shane   He won't catch any anyway.

Dave   Says who?

Shane   Says me.

Dave   Bet you I do.

Shane   Bet you you don't.

Dave   How much?

Shane   I bet you I catch something before you do.

Dave   Right.

Shane   I bet it's dead spooky down there at night, don't you?

Dave   Yea. We might see a ghost. Hey, you're fishing, right, and there's a ghost behind you with his head under his arm and you swing your rod back to cast out and hook his head.

Shane   Yea, and it goes fechew, right out into the pond. Platunge.

Trev   Look, er, Dave?

Dave   What?

Trev   Will you and Shane nip down to the shop and get us a tin of sweet corn, just in case this stuff doesn't work?

Dave   Yea, OK. Ta. If there's any change, can I have it?

Trev   Yea.

Dave   C'on, Shane.

The boys leave, footsteps are heard receding down yard to back gate. The gate is opened, then shut.

Trev (*to* **Pogo**)   Are you all right, now?

Pogo   I think I need to use the toilet.

Trev   Come on, I'll take you home to get changed.

Trev *and* **Pogo** *leave the shed. Footsteps recede. We hear kids racing down back alleys, distant. Fade out. Fade in interior of* **Trev**'*s house, the landing at the top of the stairs. We are near the bathroom and can hear from inside a radio playing, a shower attachment being used to rinse hair.* **Cassie** *is singing along to the music, quietly.*

Voice (*from bottom of stairs*)   Cassie! Don't waste all the water, your dad wants a bath.

The noise of shower, music and singing continue.

Malc (*very close*)   Cassie. Cassie. It's me, Malcolm. I'm in my bedroom. Can you hear me? Please hear me. Feel my love for you reaching out. I'm sending my brain waves out to you. They're in the street. They're coming through your letter box and up your stairs, under your bedroom door. I'm in your room. I'm beside you. Don't be scared. It's just a close encounter.

Brushing his teeth.

I love you. Malcolm Panks loves Cassandra Buckfield. Think of me. Think 'Malcolm is all right. He's a good kid.' Think, 'I could love him if I tried.'

Spitting out toothpaste in bowl.

Cassie, I've got one of your butterfly clips for your hair. With it being so close to you I can use it to help project myself into your head. I am now going to kiss it.

Kissing noise.

Can you feel me kissing you? Oh, Cassie, please be my
girlfriend again. I won't take you up the Golden Nuggett
again, not if you don't want to go.

Cassie *opens the bathroom door. Music louder. She brings the radio with
her along the landing and into her bedroom. The noise from the radio is
beginning to drown out* **Malc**'s *astral projected voice. We follow her into
the bedroom.*

If you go out with me, I'll stop playing the machines. I'll pack
it in, I promise. I'll do whatever you want. Look, Maurice
doesn't love you, not like I do – Hang on, my mum's shouting
me. I'll just go and see what she wants.

A new record begins on the radio. **Cassie** *turns it up.*

Trev (*from bottom of stairs*)   Cassie! Turn it down!

Cassie *turns on her hair dryer.* **Trev** *comes up the stairs, knocks on
door, comes in.*

Your mam says turn it down!

Cassie   What? (*Turns off hair dryer.*)

Trev (*turning off the radio*)   Mam says to turn it down.

Cassie   Down's not off. (*Turns on hair dryer.*)

Trev   Where you going?

Cassie   Out.

Trev   Oh.

Cassie   You won't put me off him.

Trev   OK.

Cassie   I don't tell you what to do, do I? Who to go out
with?

Trev   No. I'm a lot older than you, though.

Cassie   So? You're nothing to do with me.

Trev   I care about you. So does my dad.

Cassie   Why?

Trev   Why do you think?

Cassie   He married my mum, that's all. I wasn't part of it. I don't want you thinking you have to look after me.

Trev   I don't have to.

Cassie   I don't need you. I managed before I knew you. I'm old enough to look after myself. I'm not a baby. I'm not daft.

Trev   Look, just be careful, I –

The hair dryer is turned off.

Cassie   What is it about Maurice, eh? What have you got against him? What's he supposed to have done? (*Pause.*) I don't care what he's done. I know what he's like. He's a laugh. He's not boring like you and everyone else round here. (*Pause.*) It's a show. Don't you think I know that? It's all a show. But I don't mind. You just don't know him like I do.

Trev   I've known him a hell of a lot longer than you.

Cassie   And that means you understand him? Big brother – understands everybody. Wants to run everybody else's life for them. You want to look at your own. What do you do, eh? What do you do?

Pause.

Malc (*very close*)   It's me again. She wanted me to open the sauce bottle. She's got a dead weak grip. She says it's from wringing out all them wet clothes. We only got a proper spinner last year. I've got to have my tea now and then I'm off out with your Trev, so I'll get back to you tonight when we're both in bed. Love you. (*Kiss blown.*)

We hear the radio on, loud. Then the radio off.

Trev   I haven't finished.

Cassie   Just leave my stuff alone, will you? You're not telling me what to do. Get out! go on, get out. This is my room. Do you mind getting out of my room?

Trev   It used to be my room.

Cassie   Well it's mine now. Go on, go and play with your floats.

Trev   Look, Cassie. I'm just trying to make you see sense. All I'm saying is –

Cassie   You're not saying anything! You haven't told me anything!

Trev   I want you to take care, Cassie. I like Maurice. I like him. Vic and me and Maurice – we were mates. More me and Vic really, 'cos Maurice was younger, but he always used to be there, he'd tag along wherever we went. (*Pause.*) Look, his brother, Vic – he's away – because of a girl.

Cassie   What? (*Pause.*) Well what's that got to do with Maurice? (*Pause.*) What did he do?

Trev   Something happened with this girl. He got sent away. It finished their family. Kids at school used to shout things about Vic, and Maurice would go berserk – I mean really crazy – even big kids in the fifth year, when he knew he'd just get hammered back. He's eaten up with it, Cassie. It's kind of sent him a bit rotten inside.

Cassie   No, Trevor. He's not. (*Pause.*) Who was the girl?

Trev   That's not important. Don't think I'm trying to split you up. I just want you to understand. (*Pause.*) I think you've done this room lovely. Much better than when I had it.

Trevor *leaves. In a moment* **Cassie** *puts on the hair dryer again. Fade out.*

Fade in exterior: the ponds. The tranquillity is broken, the gang are setting up on the bank – tackle boxes opened, rummaging, wicker baskets opened, creaking. Bait box lids off. Lines wound on reels, the clicking of the reel clutches.

Dave   Oh! I can't get my line threaded through these rings!

Shane   You've missed one out.

Trev   I'll help you in a minute. Let me finish Pogo's.

Dave   I want to get started!

Shane   Where's my reel?

Pogo   Don't be in such a rush – eh, Trev?

Trev   Don't stamp about on the bank, Shane, I've told you, you'll scare the fish off. (*He begins to help* **Pogo** *with her tackle.*)

Shane   Who's stamping?

Dave   You're treading in the bait!

Shane   Have you got my reel? Lift up, Dave, let me have another look in the basket.

Pogo   Did you see that?

Trev   What?

Pogo   I saw something.

Dave (*to* **Shane**)   What are you doing? That's the sandwich box.

Trev   Where?

Pogo   Out there.

Dave   You did put it in the basket, didn't you?

Shane   I thought you did. Oh, no.

Trev   What was it?

Dave (*calling*)   What you seen?

Pogo   It's gone now.

Shane   What you doing, Dave?

Dave   I'm hungry.

Shane   Help us find that reel, don't just sit there stuffing your face.

Dave (*through a mouthful of sandwich*)   I'm waiting for Trev to tie my hook on. There's supposed to be some big pike in here, int there, Trev?

Trev   Supposed to be.

Dave   They've got amazing teeth. Have you ever seen their teeth? There were some gippos caught one once and they smashed it up on a fence post. We had a look at it after they'd gone, didn't we?

Shane   I wasn't there.

Dave   You were, weren't you?

Shane   No.

Dave   Its teeth were like needles.

Pogo   This wasn't a pike. This was a Golders Green yellow submarine.

Dave   Eh? Shall I chuck a bit of sandwich in, see if it comes up for it? (*Germanic accent.*) 'Periscope up. Ah, beetroot sandwich'.

Shane   Chuck in one of them cakes not made with Bero that makes ducks sink. Chuck one of them in. 'Achtung, a depth charge! Himmel! Dive! Dive!'

Trev   Just get tackled up, will you? Keep still and keep quiet.

Shane   I can't find that reel you lent me.

Dave   He forgot to put it in the basket.

Pogo   You're making too much noise. You have to keep quiet when you're fishing, don't you, Trev?

Dave   You're an expert, are you, Pogo?

Pogo   I'm going to be.

Trev   Just shut it.

Shane   I'm going to have to go back and get it. Come with us.

Dave   I'm not. You go.

Shane   Oh, come on.

Dave   Trev?

Trev   What?

Dave   Put my hook on for us.

Trev   In a minute.

Pogo   He's doing mine, first, you'll have to wait.

Dave   Pogo.

Pogo   What?

Dave   Shut up.

Trev   Chuck some ground bait in for us, Dave. Get the catapult and just belt out a few free offerings. Little balls of ground bait.

Shane   Int nobody coming with us, then?

Dave   In a bit. Let me catch something first. Where, Trev?

Trev   In line with each rod.

Dave *fires catapult. Plop.*

Dave   About there?

Trev   A bit further.

Trev *finishes tying* **Pogo**'s *hook on. He moves to* **Dave**'s.

Dave *fires catapult. Plop.*

Pogo   Come on, Nessie, come and pick up all the tasty morsels.

Pogo *begins to sing the* Jaws *theme.* **Dave** *joins in. She plays it on the kazoo.*

Trev   Keep it quiet, you two.

We hear the creaking of wicker basket.

Dave   Oh my bum's sore on this! I should have brought a cushion.

Pogo   I spy with my little eye . . .

Dave   Something beginning with . . . T.

Pogo   Torch.

Dave   No.

Shane   Tackle box.

Dave   You aren't playing.

Pogo   Trumpet.

Dave   Eh?

Pogo *plays 'Colonel Bogey' on imaginary trumpet.*

Trev   Settle down.

Pogo   I'm sorry, Trev, I'm getting excited.

Pause.

Shane   Dave?

Dave   What?

Shane   I thought you were supposed to be my mate?

Pause. **Pogo** *begins* Jaws *theme again. It builds up, then –*

Pogo   What's that? Ssssh.

A crashing through the undergrowth.

Malc   Hiya!

Pogo   Oh, Malcolm!

Malc   What's up? Hey, don't point that catapult at me.

Trev   Hi, Malc.

Malc   How you doing?

Trev   Still setting up.

Shane   I'm off back on my own, then.

Dave   Oh, come on, then! Look after my rod for us, Malc. Don't catch anything, though, leave it for when I come back, right?

Malc   Yea, sure.

Dave *and* **Shane** *leave, move off along the track.* **Malc** *settles down on the basket vacated by* **Dave**.

Malc   It's great here, isn't it? When it's like this, starting to get dark. Stars coming out. Stillness. It's like a different world. It's as though you're in one of them cathedrals where you have to talk quiet.

Trev   Sometimes, it's so quiet after the sun's gone down, you can hear the carp right out in the middle when they come up to the surface for bits of food. A kind of gentle slurping noise. Just a mouth closing round a bit of floating crust and you can hear it magnified in the darkness.

Pause. They listen. A still sunset.

Malc   Last time I came here at night I chucked some books in.

Trev   What?

Malc   Some mucky books. My mam found them in my bedroom. They were on the tea table when I came in from school. She made me feel like a sex pervert.

Pogo   You are. We all know what Malcolm Panks is. All you men are, aren't they, Nessie? They're all sex maniacs. Can't you talk about anything else?

Pause.

Malc   She wouldn't let me put them in the dustbin in case the dustbin man found them. I had to get rid of them at night, in the dark. So I got a sack out the coal shed and put them in that and came down here. I put some stones in and cobbed it out into the pond.

Pause. In the distance we hear **Dave** *and* **Shane** *doing werewolf howls.*

Pogo   What's that?

Trev   It's our Dave turning into a werewolf.

Malc   Why I came here that night, it's like I suppose I was saying sorry – you know – confessing a sin. 'Cos God, he hangs around in places like this, don't you reckon? If he hangs around anywhere.

Pogo   Well he's not in the Golden Nuggett, is he?

Malc   No, I don't reckon. He'd have given me fifty p.

Pogo   He could be, though. He could have come down to earth and be in disguise as somebody playing the machines.

Malc   Highest score this month – God, twelve thousand nine hundred and eighty-nine.

Pogo   I think what you said before, though, about him being here. He could be. He could be the carp.

Trev   We'd better pack in, then? God's not going to let himself get caught, is he?

Malc   No.

Pause.

Pogo   Jesus did.

Pause

Malc   That star reflection, down there. That could be him.

Pause.

Trev   It's like fishing in the universe.

Pause.

Malc   Trev?

Trev   What?

Malc   You know when you get older – do you, like, understand things better?

Trev   No.

Pause.

Malc   Well what happens, then?

Trev   You just have more things you can't understand.

Pause.

Malc Oh. Is that why you come fishing? (*Pause.*) I don't want to get older.

Trev Who does?

Pogo Me. I do. You give me your years if you don't want them.

Malc My mam says she still feels sixteen in her head. But she can't do. I mean, she never has a laugh or owt. Do you still feel sixteen?

Trev No.

Malc No. You sort of act like someone in their twenties.

Trev I am.

Malc Yea. It's weird, innit?

Pause.

Pogo (*singing, quietly*) Twinkle twinkle little star
 How I wonder what you are . . .

Fade out on song.

Fade in exterior: back alley with high walls which give a slight echo to **Dave** *and* **Shane***'s footsteps as they come towards us.*

Shane When his hands started rippling and growing all them hairs.

Dave Yea, and his jaw came right out. It was ace, wasn't it?

They demonstrate turning into werewolves and fight.

Dave Aah!

Shane What's up?

Dave You just poked your finger in my eye.

Shane Sos.

Dave I can't see. Right in my eyeball.

Shane Sos. Sos Dave.

Dave   That bloody hurt.

Shane   I said I'm sorry.

Dave   You dip-head.

Shane   Yea – well – it hurt me when you bit my neck before. What am I going to tell my mam? Dave Buckfield give me a love bite?

Dave *runs at* **Shane**, *they have a friendly fight.*

Dave   Aah! What's that?

Shane   What?

Dave   I've just hit something hard on your leg. What is it?

Shane   Nowt.

Dave   What you got on?

Shane   Eh?

Dave   Let's have a look.

Shane   Get off!

Dave   You've got stockings on!

Shane   I haven't.

Dave   You have. What's that, a suspender belt?

Shane   No.

Dave   Yes it is, you've got stockings on!

Dave *falls about laughing.*

Shane   I'm going home.

Dave   Didn't your mum have any tights?

Shane   She would only lend me these. She thinks I'm using them to net tiddlers. My dad uses them sometimes for making wine.

Dave *is hysterical.*

I'm going home. I'm going home if you're laughing. Don't tell.

Don't tell anybody, Dave.

They begin to move on again up the alley.

Dave What do they feel like?

Shane They feel all right.

Dave What, sexy?

Shane Yea, a bit.

Dave Hey, what if you'd have got knocked over coming round to our house?

They reach the back gate, open it.

Shane I know, I was thinking that.

They walk up yard and go into shed.

Dave There's a light switch here somewhere.

Click.

Oh. We've come for a reel. He forgot it.

There is a scuffling, of people getting up.

Cassie Oh.

Dave It's in here, somewhere. Look for it, then, Shane. We didn't think anyone was in here.

Cassie Well there is.

Dave Yes. Hello, Maurice.

Shane I've found it. Come on.

Maurice I know you, don't I?

Shane No.

Cassie What's up?

Maurice I know him.

Cassie So?

Maurice Don't I?

Shane   No.

Dave   What's going on?

Cassie   Come on, Maurice, let him out.

Maurice   I never forget a face. Can you remember where it was? Last night? Didn't I see you last night?

Dave   He was down at the ponds last night. He was watching a bloke fishing, weren't you?

Maurice   Watching what?

Shane   I was watching a bloke fishing.

Maurice   All night? You weren't watching something else?

Cassie   Leave him, Maurice, let him go, now. Don't frighten him.

Maurice   You're a good runner, aren't you?

Shane   No.

Maurice   You're a little jack rabbit.

Dave   He's my mate. Tell him, Cassie, tell him to pack it in.

Cassie   Maurice.

Maurice   This little jack rabbit was out in the woods last night.

Pause. A sniffle from **Shane**.

Cassie   Was it him?

Shane   I didn't see anything.

Cassie   There was nothing to see.

Shane   I know.

Maurice   You enjoy it do you, watching in the woods? Exciting?

Shane   No.

Maurice   Just a hobby, is it? Like train spotting? You got a notebook and pencil?

Dave Leave him, Maurice, please. He's my mate. He didn't mean anything. He won't do it again, will you?

Maurice Did we get a five star rating?

Cassie He doesn't understand, Maurice. He doesn't understand what you're on about. Leave it now, come on, I don't want to listen to any more.

Maurice You like girls, eh?

A sob.

Dave (*to* **Cassie**) Do summat!

Shane They're all right.

Maurice Do you know what you are? Eh?

Shane Yes.

Maurice What?

Cassie I'm going. Let me out.

Maurice What!?

Pause.

Shane A pervert.

Cassie He doesn't mean anything. He's just a kid. He's just a kid, Maurice, don't take it out on him.

Maurice What? What you on about? Don't take what out on him?

Cassie I don't know.

Maurice Don't take what out on him? We let him get away with it then? We let him go.

Pause. **Maurice** *moves aside. The boys rush out and down the yard.*

Trevor's told you, hasn't he? Clever Trevor.

The boys are in the alley now. Their shouts echo.

Dave   You friggin maniac bully! You're piggin sick! (*Pause.*)
You want your head boiled in Dettol! It's you that's a perv,
you're sick! They all are in your family. You're a nut! A nut
cracker. A barmy bullying . . .

Shane   Lump of dog's diarrhoea!

Dave   Yea!

Shane   I hope somebody gets your nuts and cracks them!

Dave   Yea! In a vice! And then sticks a red hot poker up
your nose and welds all your snot to your brain.

They are a little closer now, gaining in confidence.

Shane   What brain? He ant got a brain.

Dave   My brother's gonna get you tommorer. You'd better
get out of his shed. You're gonna get done, you wait. You're
gonna get smacked by our Trev! He'll smash your head in.
You're gonna get hammered. (*To* **Shane**.) C'on.

Shane   I'm off home. (*Runs off up the alley.*)

Dave   Oh come on! Come on, Shane.

Shane   No.

Pause.

Maurice   What did he tell you?

Cassie   He was on about what Vic did. (*Pause.*) He told me
who the girl was. (*Pause.*) It was Pogo, wasn't it?

Silence.

Fade in exterior: the ponds. We arrive back with **Trev**, **Pogo** *and*
Malc *as if from high above them. We can faintly hear the last verse of*
'Summer Nights' being sung in something approaching harmony by **Pogo**
and **Malc**. *We come down closer as they get to the end of the song . . .*

Those summer Ni . . . hights

Trev (*singing*)   Tell me more, tell me more.

A gentle laugh, the sound of friends together. Pause.

Malc   I like moths. He keeps knocking himself out, down here. Why do moths fly to the light?

Pause.

Pogo   Maybe they're afraid of the dark.

Malc   When you catch one and cup it in your hands, it sort of tickles as it walks about inside. And when you open your hands they stay there for a bit, not sure what to do, don't they? They're like waiting for permission to be set free.

Pause.

Pogo   I still sleep with the curtains open because my mum once said God put stars in the sky to stop us being afraid of the dark.

Malc   I used to be. Did you Trev?

Trev   I can't remember.

Malc   You grow out of all that.

Pause.

Pogo   Trev, can I reel in to see if my bait's still on? It might have come off. Can I check it?

Trev   If you want.

We hear the clicking of a fixed spool reel.

Malc   Oh no.

Trev   What?

Malc   Oh no. I knew this would happen. It's doing it, the line's moving. Look!. My bit of silver paper's jigging about on the line . . . Oooooh. (*Strikes rod.*) Oh no! I've caught summat! There's summat on, here.

Trev   He's got one!

Pogo   Woahhh. Mine! Mine's going! Strike!

Malc   Oh bloody bananas, I've got summat here.

Pogo's *speech overlaps the dialogue between* **Malc** *and* **Trev**.

Trev Just take it easy, both of you. Keep the rod up, Malc.

Malc What is it? A carp or a pike?

Trev I don't know.

Malc It feels like an octopus on heat.

Pogo Now then, let it run, or it'll snap the line.

Let the rod do all the work.

It's going like a train, mine. Let the train take the strain.

Pogo It's not now. It's not going like a train. (*Pause.*) It's coming in like a wet sack, Trev.

Malc So is mine, Trev. It's coming in like a wet sack, Trev.

Trev Let me get the landing net. Hold your rod up, let me get right underneath.

Trev *gets the net in the water and the 'catch' is hauled out onto the bank.*

Malc What is it? What we got? What is it, Trev?

Pogo You've got mine in there too.

Trev Yes. That's because you've caught each other, and half a ton of weed.

Malc Is that all? I had a fish, didn't I?

Trev Pogo's line must have caught yours when she reeled in. No fish.

Malc Oh, great. Thanks, Pogo, I nearly had a heart attack 'cos of you.

Pogo Go on, say it. I know you think I'm incontinent.

Malc Eh?

Pogo You, you mean. You're incompetent.

Trev Go and look after my rod, Pogo, while I untangle this lot.

Pogo *moves across to* **Trev**'s *spot.*

Pogo   You shouldn't have been fishing so close.

Malc   I didn't cast in!

Trev   Pack it in, you two!

Pause.

Pogo   I'm not conversing any more.

Malc   Do you want some help?

Trev   Yea, you hang on to that end.

Malc   You'll have to cut the line.

Pause.

Trev   Pass your end under there.

Pause. An accelerating clicking from **Trev**'s *rod.*

Pogo!

Pogo *strikes, the line tightens, singing as the big fish makes its first run.* **Trev** *and* **Malc** *rush over.*

Pogo   Now then have I got her? Eh? What's this, then, a dead donkey? It's Nessie, this is. Nessie. What did I say? I said, didn't I? Just keep the rod high, Pogo, let the rod do all the work. That's it, good girl. I told you we'd get her, eh, Trev? I can do it! Let me do it! She's going . . . she's moving down, I can feel her going deeper. (*The clicking reel slows.*) She's slowing down. (*Clicking stops.*) She's stopped on the bottom, Trev. I can't move her. (*Pause.*) Blip. (*Pause.*) Blip. Yellow submarine.

Trev   Don't try to reel in, you'll snap off. Just hold, just wait. (*Pause.*) Keep the tension, don't drop the rod end. She'll move in a minute.

Pogo   She's working out what to do next. Keep the tension. Let her do all the work. She's just having a rest.

Trev   It's all open water here. When she goes, just let her go. There's only some reeds on this side. If she makes a bolt for them put some side strain on, make her turn into open water.

Click. Click.

Pogo She's going! (*Clicking accelerates.*) She's going! We're off again! (*The line is singing as it cuts through the water.*)

Malc I think it is the Loch Ness monster.

Pogo Yipee! 'Thar she blows!'

Trev Watch what you're doing! Watch it!

Pogo I know, I know.

Trev You're doing great. If the hook's well in her lip, she's yours.

Malc Could the hook come out?

Trev Sometimes they pull the bend in the hook straight.

Malc What, a fish?

Trev A big fish like this. Sometimes the hook snaps.

Pogo Shut up, will you? Shut up! Come on girl, that's it. She's turning. She's tiring. Come on, girl, come on, Nessie. Oh, Trev, she feels fantastic. I can feel all the power of her body through the line.

Malc Come on, Nessie.

Trev Come on, Nessie, come on, girl. That's it.

Malc Can you see owt, yet?

Trev Get the net, get the landing net, Malc!

Malc (*running across*) It's better than space invaders, this.

Pogo Don't let me lose her now. Not now, please. I'll be good, I promise. Just let me see her, let me hold her. I won't keep you. I'll let you go. I won't hurt you.

Malc *stumbles back.*

Trev The landing net, not the keep net!

Malc *races back.*

Keep her coming in, steady, bring her up.

Malc Here.

The net goes out waiting for **Pogo** *to bring the fish over the top. Splashing.* **Trev** *wades out a little way.*

Trev   Oh, man, look at this, she's under. She's ours.

The fish is in the net. **Trev** *begins to haul it up on to the bank.*

Malc   Oh, man, it's amazing.

Trev   It must weigh more than fifteen pounds.

Pogo   Have I done it?

Trev   Look.

Pogo   I can't. Have I hurt her?

Trev   No. I'm taking the hook out.

Pause. The fish flaps, then stops. Silence whilst the delicate operation of removing the hook is performed.

It's out.

Pogo   Can I look?

Trev   Yes. (*Pause.*) Does that make it your best summer?

Malc   Who's the champion of Decoy Ponds then, eh?

Pogo   She's lovely.

Malc   The biggest fish ever caught from here, and you caught it.

Trev   What's wrong?

Pogo   She doesn't like it out here, Trev, she wants to go back. Let's put her back now.

Trev   Let me weigh her first.

Pogo   No, I don't want to. We know it's Nessie, we don't need that. Please put her back now, Trev.

Trev   It's your fish.

Pogo   I think we ought, don't you, Malcolm?

Malc   I've never seen anything like this.

Pogo She belongs to the pond. She wants to slide slowly away, down into the deep water, doesn't she, Trev? Back to the star. Her eye – it's telling us.

Trev Come on, we'll let you go.

Trev *picks up the fish and makes his way into the water where he lays the fish, supported by his hands.*

Malc She won't go. She's waiting for permission.

A swirl in the water and the fish makes off.

Trev There. Gone back now. (*He wades out and falls onto the bankside.*) That was . . . (*Inhales, blows out, noisily.*)

Pogo Yea . . . (*She does the same.*)

Malc Yea, it was a bit . . . (*Does same.*) wasn't it?

They fall about laughing, the tension gone.

Champion Pogo!

Pogo (*singing*) Champion the wonder horse, fish I mean.

Trev You did it, you really did it.

They do a little jig.

Pogo You can kiss me if you like, Trev.

Trev *gives her a noisy kiss.*

Malcolm?

Malc No thanks, I might turn into a frog.

Pogo *chases him.*

Pogo Come here and be loved.

She catches him and smothers him in kisses.

Malc Ribbett! Ribbett! I'm suffocating!

Trev Hang on to him, Pogo, he might jump in the pond.

Malc (*amourously*) Oh, I wish you were Cassie.

Trev Oh, no.

Pogo (*getting off him*)   Oh, no.

Malc (*shouting into the night, across the water*)   Cassie! I love you! It's me, Malcolm, can you hear me?

Pogo   Can you hear him, Cassie? Yooooohoooooo. Cassie.

Malc   Over the misty lake to my beloved!

Trev   Hurry up and answer before we drown him!

Malc   Oh lady of the lake! (*Yodelling.*) O Lady of the La-a-ke. (*Close.*) Eh, Pogo?

Pogo   What?

Malc   You're the Lady of the Lake, now, aren't you?

Pogo   Am I? What's that, then?

Malc   It's a legend.

Pogo   What about? Fish?

Malc   Knights in armour and damsels in distress.

Pogo   Which am I?

Pause.

Malc   Cassie's a damsel in distress. I'm off to get a twelve foot lance – about as long as this rod – and I'm off to shove it right up Maurice Edlington's arse!

They all laugh. It echoes out across the water into the night. Fade out.

Interior: the shed. Fade in on **Trevor**'s *tape being played.* **Trev**'s *'Bridge Over Troubled Water' song. It continues quietly, in the background.*

Pogo   I caught a fish last night. Did he tell you? (*Pause.*) He's got another think coming if he thinks I'm going to miss him. (*Pause.*) I don't need a bodyguard, you know, Cassie, you don't have to stay. Do you think I'm going to steal something from the shed?

Cassie   Do you want me to go?

Pogo   It won't take me long to forget him. I'll soon forget him, just like I forget everything else. What time did he go?

Cassie   Early.

Pause. **Pogo** *switches off the tape in the middle of the song. Pause.*

Pogo (*singing, softly to herself*)

One two three four five,
Once I caught a fish alive.
Six seven eight nine ten
then I put it back again.

Trevor helped me to keep it all together. He'll be coming back, though, won't he? Going away and coming back. Just visiting. Passing through. Fragments. Everything. It goes away. Why does it all float away? (*Pause.*) When I have to go to the hospital for the last time, will I have forgotten everything? Will it be like a blank tape?

Cassie   You'll remember Trevor.

Pogo   Why?

Cassie   Because he loves you.

Pogo   Yes. I'll remember I love Trevor and Trevor loves me. And I love my mum and dad and they love me. And I love Jesus and he loves me. They'll probably all get mixed up so I think my dad is Jesus and Trevor is my mum. But I'll have the love, won't I? That will be there. I probably won't remember where it came from, but I can take it with me, can't I? I can take it with me when I go to meet Jesus and give it back to him – 'cos it all came from him in the first place, didn't it?

Pause.

Cassie (*distressed*)   I don't know. We're doing about drugs in RE.

Pause. **Pogo** *sings 'One, two, three four five . . .' We hear the back gate open and footsteps in the yard.* **Malc** *steps in.*

Malc   Hiya Pogo.

Pogo Hello Malcolm.

Cassie *gets up and rushes out, crying.*

Malc What's up with her? What's she crying for?

Pogo Her and Maurice have finished.

Malc Have they?

Pogo Last night.

Malc Really?

Pogo Yes. Go on.

Malc What?

Pogo Ask her to go out with you.

Malc Do you think I should?

Pogo Go on.

Malc I can't. I'm all sweaty. (*Sniffs.*) I could do with some roll on. Wish me luck, then.

Pogo Good luck.

Malc I'll let you know what happens.

Malc *leaves. Footsteps receding up the yard.* **Pogo** *puts the tape on again. We hear the rest of* **Trev***'s song. When it ends it cuts suddenly into the middle of a recording from a Radio One programme, something like 'Power of Love', Frankie Goes to Hollywood – with DJ chat over, then just the song. Slow fade.*

The Mortal Ash

Characters

Cath Wheatley, *forty-six*
Tom Wheatley, *forty-eight*
Duane Wheatley, *seventeen*
Chris Wheatley, *twenty-three*
Rainy Wheatley, *twenty-one*
Linda Clay, *twenty-two*, (*Chris's girlfriend*)

Time   Now. Summer.

Setting   Back yard and kitchen of a council house on an estate in a South Yorkshire town.

The Mortal Ash was first performed at the Bush Theatre on 14 September 1994, with the following cast:

Tom	Paul Copley
Cath	Jane Cox
Rainy	Jane Hazlegrove
Duane	James Hooton
Linda	Colleen Prendergast
Chris	Richard Standing

Directed by Simon Usher
Designed by Anthony Lamble
Lighting by Kevin Sleep
Sound by Paul Bull

Act One

Scene One

The yard. A Saturday in summer, around mid-day. The back of the council house is visible. **Catherine** *can be seen at the kitchen window. From somewhere at the front of the house we can hear* **Chris** *tapping out broken glass from a window in readiness to replace it.*

The yard is mainly hard earth. A flat area of about eight foot by six foot has darker coloured soil. This is where the old bird aviary stood. In the centre of this area is a small mound of soil, with stones surrounding it. There is an old shed to one side, next to an arched brick alleyway which separates this house from the next. It is a well-used back yard. The grass is parched and thin, where it hasn't been concreted over. A couple of dustbins stand under the kitchen window, bits of old wood lie about. **Duane** *is sat on a home made bench, some-way down the yard.* **Catherine** *comes out to put some kitchen waste in the dustbin.*

Cath You can sulk all day, Duane, I've told you you're not having one.

Duane But he's bringing me the wood this afternoon.

Cath Well you can just get round and tell him not to bring it, then, can't you?

Duane It weren't costing owt.

Cath I don't care. You're not having a bird aviary. You didn't even ask.

Duane I forgot.

Cath We had enough on with the last one. It were me that finished up feeding them. You never, nor your dad neither.

Duane We've allus had a bird aviary.

Cath Well we haven't now. Time I had a bit of light in

'kitchen, anyroad.

Duane   I din't want it in 'yard.

Cath   Where else can you put one?

Duane   In my bedroom.

Cath   You dozy apeth. How can you have one in your bedroom?

Duane   Why not? In 'alcove.

Cath   Bird shit everywhere. That's proper hygenic, that is. Be thankful for what you've got.

Duane   What have I got?

Cath   You'll get it when your dad gets in. That's apart from all 'baking I'm doing. You want to be thankful. When I were your age, only cake we ever got were 'windmill cake.

Duane   If it goes round, you get a bit. Yea, I know.

Cath   You've done very well, my lad, as it is, without wanting more.

Pause.

Duane   It were good wood. He's not using it for owt. There were enough to make loads of stuff.

Cath   Like what?

Duane   I don't know. A trellis. One of them rose porches.

Cath   Oh, aye, and who's going to make me that? You going to do it?

Duane   No.

Cath   Well Chris won't, he's only here once in a blue moon. And your dad can't now he's working away all week. Not that he would anyway. I'm still waiting for 'foot to be put on that tallboy in our bedroom. Been propped up with a brick for twenty years. More than that.

Duane Look nice out here. Creosote it. Like an archway. Creepers or summat growing up it.

Cath Aye. I wonder how long it'd last? Anyroad, you're not having it, so be said.

Duane When am I having my party?

Cath When your dad gets in.

Chris *comes out of the house eating a sausage roll.*

Chris I need a chisel to get putty out. (*To* **Duane**.) Are you going to help me with this glass?

Cath I'll help you. He's going out. (*To* **Duane**.) And don't bring any more stones back. I'm getting plenty as it is, by special delivery. Enough for a bloody rockery soon. That's what you can mek me if you're stuck for summat to do. Now get yourself off and tell him thanks but no thanks. (*To* **Chris**.) And you stop eating them sausage rolls, I'll have none left. (*She goes in.*)

Chris Where you off?

Duane Jeff Hicks.

Chris You what?

Duane Jeff Hicks.

Chris What for?

Duane He were giving me some wood. She says I can't have it.

Chris She says right.

Duane Why?

Chris What you doing seeing him?

Duane I've seen him around a bit.

Chris I thought you'd have more sense.

Duane It's only some he din't want. I were looking at it. He said I could have it for nowt.

Chris　You been hanging around his place?

Duane　Yea.

Chris　What's he wanna be giving you wood for? What's he after?

Duane　Nowt.

Chris　Peace offering, is it?

Duane　You what?

Chris　Stay away.

Duane　Sod off. I'll go where I want. What's it got to do wi' you? Just 'cos you don't like him.

Pause.

Chris　You've been in his barn, then?

Duane　Yea. It's like a junk yard, all the gear he's got. Dead old, some of it. You been in?

Chris　Years ago.

Duane　Massive, innit? Fit our house in it about six times. Beams on it. Dead thick. He says there's owls.

Chris　Used to be.

Duane　It's ace. Yonks old. He were on about where name comes from.

Chris　Oh, aye?

Duane　Did you know?

Chris　Course I know. Everybody knows.

Duane　What, then?

Chris　Tree where they used to hang people.

Duane　Yea, but do you know what they used to do wi' bodies after they cut 'em down?

Chris　What?

Duane Chuck 'em in 'pond.

Chris Get out.

Duane I'm telling you.

Chris Jeff Hicks told you that?

Duane Yea, I bet if they had a dig about they'd find loads of bones and stuff.

Chris Yea, cow bones, from where they've gone in for a drink and got stuck in 'mud.

Duane Human bones.

Chris Yea, well, they're not going to find out now it's all been filled in, are they?

Duane No. Might be Dick Turpin in there.

Chris Aye, Black Bess an' all.

Duane Eh, yea.

Chris He's a bullshitter.

Duane Who?

Chris Jeff Hicks.

Duane No he in't.

Chris Not much.

Duane He were saying, all them trees roun' pond, them what we used to climb and that, they're from the seeds of the proper Mortal Ash.

Chris Yea.

Duane Yea.

Chris Well there's none left now to carry on the name, is there?

Duane No, just a few pulled up stumps. (*Pause.*) That swing we 'ad. Ace, want it? Right over 'pond, let go and bomb drop right in 'middle. Remember when you and Eric had to carry me home?

Chris You don't. You were unconscious.

Duane I know. How high were I up 'rope?

Chris About twenty feet.

Duane Was I? Slipped and dropped right onto the knot, balls first.

Chris You went white, then sort of see through.

Duane It's making me ache thinking about it.

Chris Laid you out on 'kitchen table. Mam thought you were dead.

Duane I did an all.

Chris When you come round . . . puking everywhere. Never seen so much puke come out of one person.

Duane Only you.

Chris Get out.

Duane Pissed on a pint.

Chris Oh, yea, I'm sure.

Duane Are we off out tonight?

Chris Where?

Duane Pub.

Chris No.

Duane Take dad.

Chris No.

Duane Why not?

Chris No. Mam'll want us 'ere.

Duane After.

Chris No.

Duane Why not?

Chris Dad won't want to go. He'll be too knackered.

Duane He'll come for me if I ask him.

Chris If I'm going an' all?

Duane Why not? He's all right. It were just a row. He's forgot it.

Chris Yea.

Duane 'Course he has. He's been all right.

Chris What's he said about me, then?

Duane Nowt. He ant said owt.

Chris I bet.

Duane Mam said he said he's looking forward to us all being together.

Chris Yea, well she won't want us going to the pub, will she?

Duane Why not?

Chris Eric.

Duane We don't have to go to that pub.

Chris Any pub.

Duane She will.

Pause.

Chris Have you heard from Eric?

Duane No. Mam went to see him. Have you?

Chris No. Written to him a couple of times.

Duane He write back?

Chris Yes. How is he, did she say?

Duane He's getting massive. Getting muscley.

Chris   Yea.

Duane   They let them do weight training.

Chris   Yes. So I hear.

Duane   Nowt else to do. (*Pause.*) We ant told him about all this. (*He nods to the patch of earth.*) Mam said not to. Won't do him any good, will it? Only make him more upset. You ant said owt to him, have you?

Chris   No. I only knew about it today, anyway.

Duane   Came out one morning and found it all smashed to pieces. All the birds dead, 'cept a couple. Must have got away. They're all down here now. (*The circle of stones. Pause.*) Which way is Canada from here?

Chris   You what?

Duane   Last of them Canada Geese flew off from 'ponds this morning. Cleared off home. They flew over this way. Did you see 'em?

Chris   No.

Duane   They came over our house. Must be this way to Canada.

Rainy *comes in the yard, carrying a plastic bag.*

Eh, up, Rainy.

Rainy   All right? What you doing?

Duane   Nowt.

Chris   All right?

Rainy   I think I've done something to my heel.

Chris   How come?

Rainy   Walking along that bottom road. It's murder. I'll be glad when it's all done. One way or another.

Duane   She's gunna get a job at Asda's when they've built it.

Chris Eh?

Rainy I never said that.

Duane You did.

Rainy I never said definite. (*To* **Chris**.) There's a rumour that's what they'll do with it in the end.

Chris It wunt surprise me.

Duane Everybody's using it to dump stuff now.

Chris What?

Duane There were a bed in there this morning. Nearly new.

Rainy Why di'nt you bring it home?

Duane I cunt carry it.

Rainy You daft bugger.

Chris People are dumping stuff at Mortal Ash?

Duane Yea.

Chris After all that's happened?

Rainy Aye. Didn't want a dump but now they've got one, might as well use it.

Chris Jesus.

Rainy *dips in the plastic bag, fetches out a paper bag.*

Rainy Here.

Duane What?

Rainy Happy birthday.

Duane *takes the bag, fetches out some fishing floats and a cassette tape.*

Duane Fishing floats. Ace. Thanks. (*Looks at tape.*) Oh, you got it.

Chris What?

Rainy Is it the right one?

Duane Def Leppard. Yea.

Chris When you gonna get some taste?

Duane They're ace. Thanks, Rainy.

Chris You taking up fishing?

Duane Yea.

Chris How come? You used to tell me and dad it were boring.

Duane Yea well I fancy giving it another go.

Rainy Wouldn't be boring if you caught something, eh, Duane?

Duane I have caught stuff.

Rainy When?

Duane (*to* **Chris**) Haven't I?

Chris When?

Duane You know I have, don't lie.

Chris One perch in ten trips.

Duane Yea, well, Mortal Ash Pond were crap. There were nowt in.

Chris There in't now, that's for sure.

Duane Where can I go? Where wor that place we saw them massive carp?

Chris Dunno. When?

Duane When we went wi' dad that time. When we saw them donkeys doing it.

Chris I don't remember.

Duane You do. He had a massive donger.

Rainy Duane.

Duane What? He did. We all went. Where wor it?

Chris That's miles away.

Duane I'll go on 'bus.

Chris You'll be knackered by the time you get there. Lumping all the gear about.

Duane Where am I going to go, then?

Rainy Where did dad used to go?

Chris That were with 'club on 'coach. Day trip.

Duane They've got me fishing gear, haven't they?

Rainy What?

Duane For me birthday.

Rainy No.

Duane Yea, they have. Where's she hid it?

Rainy I'm not saying anything.

Duane I'll show her these. Face'll tell me.

He goes in. Pause.

Rainy So how are you, then?

Chris All right.

Rainy What you been up to?

Chris Keeping busy.

Rainy Work?

Chris While it lasts. How's your place?

Rainy Crap. 'S a job, though, innit?

Chris Would you work at Asda?

Rainy I might. Work's work. (*Pause.*) Mam told you about things?

Chris I'm fixing the window. (*Pause.*) Were you in when the brick came through?

Rainy   Watching telly. (*Pause.*) I saw Linda this morning.

Chris   In town?

Rainy   She were with her mother in Top Shop.

Chris   Did you speak?

Rainy   No, they were looking at tops.

Chris   You should have.

Rainy   Yea, well . . .

Chris   She's all right, her mam. (*Pause.*) She is. I know you think she hates us, but she dunt. You're not gunna find out if you keep avoiding 'em, are you?

Rainy   No.

Chris   Well, then.

Rainy   I know. I know.

Chris   Linda's all right with you, in't she?

Rainy   Yea. I were talking to her 'other week on 'market.

Chris   She said.

Rainy   Did she get them net curtains she were after?

Chris   Yea.

Rainy   I bet it looks nice now. Sounds like it was a right dump you moved in to.

Chris   It was.

Rainy   I'm still waiting for me invite.

Chris *looks a bit sheepish.*

Chris   You'll have a long wait.

Rainy   Why?

Chris   Don't say owt.

Rainy What?

Chris We're not there any more.

Rainy Why? What's happened?

Chris Don't say owt to mam for Christ's sake. I'll never hear the last of it.

Rainy I won't.

Chris I couldn't afford 'rent any more after they put me back on basic. Wi'out overtime I'm getting bugger all.

Rainy So where are you?

Chris Her mam's for 'time being.

Rainy After all you've done to it.

Chris I know. Put a few quid in the place.

Rainy Put a few hours and all. Painting and what have you.

Chris Yea, well, if I ant got rent, I ant got it. Her mam's all right about us being there.

Rainy You'll have to say summat. If mam finds out from somebody else . . .

Chris Yea, I know. Gunna cheer her up, in't it, me being round there.

Rainy Can't be helped.

Chris Can't come back here, can I?

Rainy It's up to you.

Chris Can you see it working? I can't.

Rainy Maybe you should have taken that cottage when it were offered.

Chris No way.

Rainy I know, but . . . rent free an' all.

Chris I don't want no favours from Hicks. Done enough

for us. Set it all up, walks away clean as a whistle and we get all this.

Rainy   We? Where were you?

Chris   You know what I mean. Shit doesn't stick to money.

Rainy   Yea well when you've got none, beggars can't be choosers.

Chris   I'd live in a cardboard box before I'd go cap in 'and to that bastard.

Rainy   I'll get you one from work.

Chris   We'll sort summat out. I'm gunna be looking round for another job anyway. They've already laid off a load. I might be next.

Duane *comes out, eating a sausage roll, carrying an empty margarine tub.* **Cath** *follows him out.*

Cath   How long we got air conditioning for?

Chris   What?

Cath   Are you putting 'glass in, or what?

Chris   Yes.

Cath   You'll need 'key. (*She holds it out for him.*)

Chris   What you locked it for?

Cath   Never mind what I've locked it for. (*She gives him the key. To* **Duane**.) You get yourself off. (*To* **Chris**.) And bring me 'key back when you've locked it. (*She goes back in.*)

Chris *unlocks the shed, goes in.* **Duane** *goes to the stone circle, begins picking up the stones, examining them, then putting them in his pockets.*

Rainy   What you doing?

Duane   Ammunition.

Rainy   You what?

Duane   In case I get ambushed again. There's one wi' a fossil on, somewhere. I'm not taking that.

Rainy   Again? What do you mean? You're not chucking stones at nobody.

Duane   They chucked 'em at me.

Rainy   Who?

Duane   Some kids this morning.

Rainy   What kids?

Duane   Useless. They never hit me once. I got one of them, though.

Rainy   Keep away from them.

Duane   They started it. Going on, and then chucking stuff. I cobbed this stone. Would have hit 'em right in the guts but they ducked and turned round, so it smacked 'em on the back of the head.

Rainy   You idiot. Why can't you just stay away? You stay away from that place! We don't want no mention of it today, do you hear? You don't say owt. Got it?

Duane   What's up?

Chris *comes out of the shed, with a chisel, and locks the door.*

It stopped 'em, didn't it? They ran off. I got this lot in case they came back. I had loads more but I used 'em for bombing a frog.

Chris   You what?

Duane   There was this massive frog down 'banking.

Chris   Did you hit it?

Duane   Na.

Rainy   Good.

Duane   Splattered it.

Rainy   Duane.

Duane   No, I didn't really. It fucked off. (*He examines a stone.*) Here. Here, look, a fossil.

Chris (*coming over to see*)   Where?

Duane   There look.

Chris   What's it a fossil of?

Duane   Eh? It's a fossil, innit?

Chris   Yea, but what of?

Duane   Dick Turpin.

Chris   Oh, yea.

Duane *puts down the stone.*

Duane   Giz chisel a minute.

Chris   What for?

Duane   Giz it. I want to make some holes. (*He takes the chisel, begins making some holes in the margarine tub top.*) I'm off to collect some worms from Hicks's farm. Get some big fat juicy ones, so I can chop 'em up.

Rainy   Duane.

Duane   They grow massive in horse shit. Big as donkeys' dongers.

Rainy   Duane!

Duane   They do live in horse shit, don't they? (*He finishes the top, gives* **Chris** *the chisel back.*) Thanks. (**Cath** *comes out. To* **Rainy**.) It is a fishing rod.

Rainy   Is it?

Duane   Yea, she told me.

Rainy   No, she didn't, liar.

Duane   Oh, bloody hell, Rainy, what have I got?

Cath (*to* **Duane**)   Eh, Inspector Morse, pack it in and get gone.

Duane What?

Cath Giving everyone 'third degree. We're not telling you, so don't waste your time.

Duane (*to* **Rainy** *and* **Chris**) See you.

He goes. **Cath** *looks at* **Chris**.

Chris I'm doing it.

Cath You'll have to wait for me now. (*To* **Rainy**.) Did you get my desecrated coconut?

Rainy Yes.

She gets it out of the plastic bag, hands it to **Cath**. **Cath** *looks at it.*

Cath You paid enough for it. Where d'you get it?

Rainy I forgot it in town. I had to get it on the corner. I'm sorry.

Cath Done now. How were they?

Rainy All right.

Cath Aye, well let that be the last time.

Rainy I will, don't worry.

Cath Why, what went on?

Rainy Nothing. They're just . . . you know.

Cath I don't want them thinking we need their shop. What we haven't got we do without. I'll be glad if they do build an Asda's and them buggers finish up wi' no custom. Did you get me gazette?

Rainy No . . . I forgot.

Pause. **Cath** *looks at* **Chris** *who is mooching about.*

Cath She must be a slave driver to you.

Chris Who?

Cath Linda. Takes you all day to put a window in our

house, but you're always doing stuff for her, so you keep saying. How does she get you to do it all? Stick a feather duster up your arse while you're hoovering?

Chris   Give over.

Cath   I bet she cracks the whip with you.

Chris   No she dunt.

Cath   It's a wonder she's let you out.

Chris   I come when I want, not when she wants.

Cath   We never see you.

Chris   I'm 'ere, aren't I?

Cath   You don't have to be. You please yourself.

Chris   Thanks.

Cath   Don't feel obliged just 'cos it's Duane's birthday.

Chris   I don't. I do what I want when I want.

Cath   Oh, we know that. (*She goes in.*)

Chris   Aren't I supposed to 'ave a life of me own?

Rainy   You should have been here sometimes.

Chris   I know. I know that. But . . . yea, when I left, maybe it weren't 'right time. How long do you have to wait before it is? Is it ever 'right time? You have to weigh up 'choices.

Rainy   Think yourself lucky you've had 'chance.

Chris   You would have been off like a shot if that last one 'd asked you. You would have done 'same.

Rainy   Would I?

Chris   You were crazy about him.

Rainy   He didn't ask, though, did he?

Chris   If he had, you would've.

Rainy He weren't gunna do that when he'd already got some other lass in tow, would he? Chatting me up on one shift, her on another. Every bugger in't place knew he were two timing but me.

Chris You're not telling me, if you met the right bloke you wouldn't have thought about leaving.

Rainy Let him sweep me off me feet?

Chris Yea.

Rainy Only kind of bloke round here wants to sweep a lass off her feet wants to do it to get her arse on the floor. The sort I want I'm not likely to meet so there's no chance of me riding off into 'sunset.

Chris What sort's that, then?

Rainy Plenty of money.

Chris Money's not everything.

Rainy No, course it in't.

Chris It in't.

Rainy It's only blokes like you who've got bugger all would say a daft thing like that. See how long it is before you two start falling out over it.

Chris We won't.

Rainy Yet.

Chris So you're staying put, then?

Rainy Looks like it.

Chris You think the same as her, then?

Rainy No. You knew she'd be like this. What else did you expect?

Chris I thought for one day, she might –

Rainy For one day you can let it go in one ear and out the other. Put up with it and say nowt. Tomorrow you're not 'ere.

Chris I wanted it to be all right.

Rainy It will be if you keep your mouth shut. Just try
not to get either of them going. Things have been so . . . I
don't want anything to start it up. (*Pause.*) I got her a paper
on my way home. There's a bit in it about Mortal Ash.
There's two kids in the infirmary with suspected meningitis.
They reckon there might be a link, with all the dumping. I
just don't want anything to spoil today.

Chris Linda's coming round.

Rainy When?

Chris This afternoon. I thought . . . by now she might've
accepted things a bit. (*Pause.*) Maybe I'll meet her off the
bus and . . .

Rainy What? Take her back? You can't do that.

Chris No. (*Pause.*) We wanted to tell her summat.

Rainy What?

Chris She's pregnant.

Rainy She in't.

Chris She is.

Rainy Oh, Chris. Brilliant. That's brilliant.

Chris Yea, I know.

Rainy Come 'ere. (*She kisses him.*) Well done. When did
you know?

Chris Couple of days ago.

Rainy Oh, it's made me go all goosey.

Chris Get out.

Rainy It's definite, then?

Chris Yea.

Rainy   You'll be – what you gunna do about a place?

Chris   We'll get somewhere.

Rainy   You'll have to.

Cath *comes out with broken glass in a dustpan. She sweeps it with handbrush into the dustbin.*

Cath   I thought you were supposed to have swept it all up? Could have gone right through somebody's slippers.

Chris   I'm doing it.

Cath *goes in.*

What's she gonna say?

Rainy   She'll be over the moon.

Chris   You reckon?

Rainy   Course she will.

Chris   Rainy, will you do something for me?

Rainy   I'm not telling her. It's for you to tell her.

Chris   I know. No, I mean, will you be here when we tell her?

Rainy   Where am I going?

Chris   Will you?

Rainy   Coward.

Chris   Thanks. (*Pause.*) I'd better get on.

He goes in the house. **Rainy** *rearranges some of the stone circle.*

Scene Two

The yard. Two hours later. Mid afternoon. **Rainy** *is sat on the bench.* **Catherine** *comes out to her.*

Cath   You're back, then.

Rainy Yes.

Cath Did you go up the river?

Rainy Yes.

Cath What did they want you to go for?

Rainy Why shouldn't they?

Cath I expect I was the topic of conversation.

Rainy No.

Cath Are they coming back here?

Rainy I don't know.

Cath Well I hope so. I've done enough tea for everybody. (*Pause.*) What did you talk about, then?

Rainy Nothing.

Cath You must have talked about summat.

Rainy Mam.

Cath What? All right, please yourself if you don't want to tell me. (*Pause.*) Did you tell her about 'window?

Rainy No.

Cath Why not?

Rainy I don't know. I didn't.

Cath Did you say owt about birds?

Rainy No.

Cath Well what did you talk about, then?

Rainy I wish you'd give her and Chris a chance.

Cath Why, what have I done now?

Rainy He loves her, Mam.

Cath I know that. I'm not saying he doesn't.

Rainy So why can't you leave them be?

Cath   When have I ever interfered?

Rainy   You make him feel bad about it.

Cath   All I know is, if things were normal he'd still be here, she'd still be at home. He left because of all this business.

Rainy   He didn't.

Cath   Come on, Rainy. Weren't they both saving like mad? Chris wouldn't give you a fart if he thought he could bottle it and sell it, add to his savings. So bloody mean with his money. Begrudged paying me lodge. Got so I wouldn't take it. Well I didn't, did I, once I knew he was saving for a deposit on a house? Then all of a sudden it all goes on rent on a poky little flat the other side of town. And you're telling me it were nowt to do with what's going on?

Rainy   He just wanted to be with her.

Cath   He wanted out of this. Taken every penny he had that flat. Coming round here to borrow his dad's gear when he can't even afford a bloody paint brush.

Rainy   Mam. He just wants to be with her.

Cath   Oh, aye. What, he's done what he's done because he can't wait to sleep with her? Is he that desperate? Anyroad, he's been sleeping with her. I weren't born yesterday.

Rainy   What do you mean?

Cath   When me and Duane went to stop at your Aunty Betty's in Mansfield them two weeks. She were round here.

Rainy   She weren't.

Cath   With your dad working away, me and Duane gone, only you to work on. Give over. I knew what went on. He couldn't look at me for a week. Couldn't do enough for me. Washing up. Never washed a plate up in his life without being told to and all of a sudden he's domesticated. I might look daft.

Rainy   It's not the same as living together.

Cath   True. I bet they're at it like rabbits.

Rainy   Mam.

Cath   Summat the matter with him. Got more hormones than Tommy Lipton's got tea leaves.

Rainy   Maybe if he hadn't gone on so much, it would have been . . . And dad'd a been a bit easier on him . . .

Cath   Oh, aye, blame him.

Rainy   They both give as much as they got. I'm just saying –

Cath   You saying it were your dad drove him out? Broke his bloody heart all this business. That was the last thing he wanted, Chris to leave like that. You've only got to look at the way he is. Like he's lost an arm. I never thought your dad would ever get old. Always so fit and strong. Now there's nothing to him, walks about like a bloody ghost that can't remember where he's meant to be or why.

Linda *comes into the yard. She carries a wrapped present.*

Oh, hello, love. Nice walk?

Linda   Yes. It were all right.

Cath   Where is he?

Linda   Is he not back?

Cath   No. He were with you, weren't he?

Linda   He went off on his own.

Cath   Why? Have you had a row?

Linda   No.

Cath   What's gone on?

Linda   Nothing. He just went off to see Duane.

Cath   Oh.

Linda   I thought he'd be back by now.

Cath   Well he's not. (*Pause.*) Do you want a cup of tea while you're waiting?

Linda   No, thanks.

Cath   I'm making one.

Linda   All right.

Cath *makes a move to go in.*

Oh. This is for Duane. It's not much. (*She hands* **Cath** *a present.*)

Cath   Oh, that's nice. Thanks, Linda.

Linda   Oh, and thank you for the tea towels and stuff.

Cath   That's all right. (*To* **Rainy**.) Do you want one?

Rainy   If you're making one I will.

Cath (*to* **Linda**)   I were going to chuck 'em out. Made me a bit more cupboard space. Have you made your mind up whether you want them sheets and blankets or what?

Linda   Well, it's nice of you, but I've just bought a duvet off the market.

Cath   Oh aye? Never got on with them things. Our Bet's got one. All they do is keep sliding off the bed. You wake up with your backside like an iceberg. Either that or you're sweating cobs.

Linda   It's ten tog.

Cath   Oh aye? Give me sheets and blankets any time. Summat to tuck in. (*Pause.*) Tea for three, then? (*She goes in.*)

Linda   Did you find Duane?

Rainy   No.

Linda   We split up. Chris went down Hicks's farm. I went up on the top road.

Rainy   I went down as far as the railway. I thought he might be digging on the embankment.

Linda   Chris'll find him, don't worry. Chris'll find him.

Rainy   I hope so.

Linda   It'll be all right.

Rainy   If they told you they were going to get him, they will. Trust him to chuck a brick and hit the only girl. (*Pause.*) It would have to be them lot, wouldn't it? Bunch of bloody hooligans. Think they're 'law and order round 'ere now. Neighbourhood Watch.

Linda   What?

Rainy   Oh aye. Didn't you know? Watch our bloody house and wait to get us. Summat else now to fire it all up again. 'All tarred wi' same brush, that family.' Won't be satisfied till they've got back at all of us.

Linda   They're after Duane for hitting a girl. That's all it is.

Rainy   No it's not. Why did they tell you, then?

Linda   They didn't tell me. I overheard 'em outside 'shop.

Rainy   Said it for your benefit.

Linda   What?

Rainy   Thought you might be interested. Pass it on.

Linda   Don't be stupid. They're not part of this. My family never wanted any of this for you. Rainy, you know that's not what they want.

Rainy   What do they want, then?

Linda   Do you think they're gunna get some kind of satisfaction out of knowing what your family's having to put up with? That won't bring her back, will it? They just want to be left alone. All my aunty and uncle want to do is to try and get through the days and nights without her, not bloody fester over what happened. I don't know why other people are angry. I don't know why. I wish I did. Who the hell cared about her round here when she was alive? Now everybody's adopted her. It's sick. So bloody lawless round 'ere. All sorts of crime going on. Then summat like this happens and 'biggest families of villains are sending flowers and weeping all over 'church. It doesn't help us. They're not doing it to help us, turning on you. It's as if summat's sick in the the world and folk put up with it till something like this happens on their doorstep and it becomes an excuse to hit back. What's happened is suddenly close, real, not on telly. It's all sick. Live outside the law all their lives then suddenly become judge and jury for 'neighbourhood. They can't get at Eric so they get at you. (*Pause.*) It's not me. It's not my family. I swear it isn't. (*Pause.*)

Rainy I'm all right at work. Don't have to think. Starts as soon as I clock off. Sitting on 'bus wondering what I'm gunna find when I get 'ome. Used to be so I couldn't get down our road wi' out summat being said. Now every bugger turns away. Sit in the house wi' telly on loud, wondering what's going on outside. Then when summat does happen . . . it's all going round in my head . . . who to blame . . . I hate Chris for being out of it, because I want out of it and can't. Eric gone, Chris gone, dad away all week . . .

Linda Chris said you'd thought about moving one bit.

Rainy I've talked to mam about it, but she won't. Why should we?

Linda You want it, though?

Rainy I never thought I'd ever want to leave this place. Mates I've had. Good laughs. Hanging about. Twagging school and bunking off down to Mortal Ash wi' lads. Sharing a ciggie. All carved us names somewhere. (*Pause.*) How can you just start again? Anyway, council won't move us, we're not priority, they said.

Cath *comes out, carrying tea things on a tray.*

Cath   Anybody want a coconut macaroon?

Linda   No thanks.

Cath *pours out the tea.*

Cath   You don't have sugar, do you?

Linda   No, thanks.

Cath *gives her a cup of tea.*

Cath   So what's Chris got the hump about, then?

Linda   Sorry?

Cath   Our Chris. Did you have words?

Linda   No, not really.

Cath   Good job I've only done salad for tea. If I know Chris, that'll be him for the day.

Linda   He just wanted to find Duane.

Cath   Oh, he's gone fishing.

Rainy   What?

Cath   The bugger sneaked back while you were all out, took all his dad's fishing gear from under 'stairs. I thought I heard him rummaging about when I were on 'toilet, but he never answered. Trying to find his birthday present, I expect. (*Pause.*) So Chris left you two to have a natter, eh? (*She gives* **Rainy** *her tea.*)

Linda   Yes.

Cath   Aye, well, I suppose now you're living together he feels he wants to be on his own now and then, eh? Only natural. You can see too much of one another.

Linda   I suppose so.

Cath   He doesn't see much of his brother these days. Doesn't do you any harm to have a break. Otherwise you might be forever arguing.

Linda   Yes.

Cath   So what did you two find to talk about, then?

Rainy (*to* **Linda**)   Her ears were burning.

Cath   Yours will be in a minute. (*To* **Linda**.) Did Chris tell you his dad's working away now?

Linda   No, what's he doing?

Cath   Cleaning out blast furnaces while they're on shut down. Glad he's got something. He'd have driven me daft mooching about 'ere. I don't know what he'll do when that's finished. Find summat, I suppose, he always does. (*Pause.*) You both need a bit of space.

Linda   Chris does what he wants.

Cath   Oh, he gets out, then?

Linda   Yes.

Cath   Oh, good.

Linda   I don't mind what he does.

Cath   Aye, well, you can trust him. Takes after his dad for that. I never had any worries on that score. If your Chris's owt like him, you won't have need to be doubting him.

Linda   I don't.

Cath   He thinks a lot about you, I know that.

Rainy   I'm off for a walk.

Cath   Where?

Rainy   I don't know till I get there. (*To* **Linda**.) You coming?

Linda   Yes.

Cath   What's all 'guided tours in aid of?

Rainy   All we're doing is going for a walk.

Cath   I thought them shoes were crippling you?

Rainy   They're all right.

Cath   Leave them be for an afternoon together, can't you? What's so important you have to go now?

Rainy   If he's taken 'fishing gear, he'll be at Mortal Ash.

Cath   So? Chris'll be with him. Won't get into no trouble if he's with him.

Rainy   If he's with him.

Cath   What's going on?

Rainy   Nowt.

Cath   Summat is. What you bothered about him for all of a sudden? He knows to keep out of trouble. I've told him often enough.

Rainy   Pity it ant sunk in.

Cath   Why, what's he done now?

Rainy   Some kids are after him.

Cath   Why?

Rainy   Does there have to be a reason?

Cath   No. The buggers don't need no excuse. Somebody allus ready to have a go. (*To* **Linda**.) You see what we have to put up with?

Linda   He chucked a brick at a girl. That's the reason.

Cath   He what?

Rainy   Thanks, Linda.

Linda   What are you letting her think it's something else for? (*To* **Cath**.) He split a girl's head open.

Cath   I don't believe it.

Rainy   He did, Mam. He told me.

Cath   A girl?

Rainy   Linda overheard some kids on about it. They said they were going to get him.

Cath (*to* **Linda**)   What did they say?

Rainy   I've told you.

Cath   What did they say?

Linda   That's all they said.

Cath   They're after him 'cos of who he is.

Rainy   No, they're not.

Cath   They don't need a bloody excuse. Being part of this family's enough. (*To* **Linda**.) Isn't it?

Linda   Here we go.

Rainy   Mam, please, leave it.

Cath   She knows what's going on. If she doesn't she ought.

Rainy   Don't, Mam.

Cath   Never mind, 'Don't Mam'. She wants telling.

Linda   I know.

Cath   Oh, do you?

Linda   Yes.

Cath   Yes, I bet you do. Bet they bloody delight in telling you. We know where all this is coming from.

Linda   If that's what you want to think.

Cath   I don't think, I know. What else am I supposed to think? Who else is there to set everybody again us? You know what's going on all right.

Linda   I know what Chris's told me, that's all.

Cath   He doesn't know the half of it.

Linda   Look, is it my family's fault Duane clouts somebody with a brick?

Cath He must have had good cause.

Linda What difference does that make? Does that make it right?

Rainy It's his own fault. Don't blame her. She's been out trying to find him for us.

Chris *comes into the yard.*

Cath Where is he?

Chris What?

Cath Duane.

Chris I dunno.

Cath Ant you been with him?

Chris No, I cunt find him.

Cath He's at Mortal Ash Ponds.

Chris I cunt see him.

Linda (*to* **Chris**) You go and find him. I'm going home.

Chris What's going on?

Cath You do what you like, lass, you have done so far.

Linda I know when I'm not wanted.

Cath I've not said I don't want you 'ere, have I?

Chris What you been saying?

Cath I can speak me mind in me own house, I hope.

Chris Thanks, Mam.

Cath So what you doing? Are you clearing off now?

Chris (*to* **Linda**) You want to go?

Linda Yes.

Cath (*to* **Chris**) Can't you make a decision for yourself these days? (*She picks up the tray.*) Oh, well, please yourself, I'm not keeping you. (*She goes in.*)

Chris What's she said?

Linda How can I tell her about the baby?

Chris What's she said?

Rainy I'll tell her.

Linda I told you she'd be like this. I knew she were still the same.

Rainy (*to* **Chris**) She shunt have come back here on her own and give her the chance. You should have gone looking together.

Chris Didn't you say owt?

Rainy Don't start at me.

Cath *comes out, putting her coat on, present in hand. She offers it to* **Linda.**

Chris What's this?

Cath We don't want it, an' I can go and find him myself.

Chris It's not for you, it's for Duane.

Cath He won't take it.

Chris What?

Rainy (*to* **Cath**) Stop it!

Chris Course he'll take it. It's fruit and nut, what's the matter with you?

Cath Is that it? A bar of bloody chocolate?

Linda (*taking it*) Thank you.

Chris Oh, you're wonderful, aren't you? What's the matter with you?

Linda It's all right, Chris, I get the message.

Chris What's the matter with you?!

Cath Don't shout at me, this is your mother you're

talking to.

Chris   And who do you think this is? Somebody I've just dragged in off the street for the afternoon?

Linda   No, I'm the girl who's taken her son away from her, aren't I?

Chris   I'm a grown man, for Christ's sake, I can –

Cath   Between your legs, not between your ears.

Chris   Jesus!

Linda   It wouldn't make a scrap of difference to you what had happened wi' my family, would it? It wouldn't matter who it was. Queen of bloody Sheba wouldn't be good enough for your son. That's top and bottom of it. All else you just make up as a reason to come between us.

Cath   Make up? Make up? I wish it were. Bloody windows, bloody birds. Eric inside.

Chris   He put himself inside. It's nowt to do wi' them. You bottle somebody in a pub, you pay the price.

Cath   Aye, it doesn't matter to you he was provoked beyond standing it any longer.

Chris   No, it doesn't, when the bloke needs fifteen stitches in his face.

Cath   Don't you think he didn't know what would happen? Don't you think he hadn't weighed all that up beforehand? How many other times had he managed to walk away from it? If he knew it'd be the end of any hope of a career in 'army, doing summat like that, when that's all he's ever wanted since he were fifteen, do you think he wasn't provoked out of all reason? The buggers wouldn't leave him be over that accident. Wouldn't. How long was he meant to take being called what he was called?

Chris   He shouldn't have done it.

Cath   It was an accident!

Chris   Bottled him, I mean.

Cath   If you can't see where this is coming from, you've been bloody well brainwashed.

Chris   You're mad.

Cath   Aye, I'm a bloody fruit and nut case.

Chris   You are.

Cath   Well if I am, we know what's made me.

She makes to go off. **Rainy** *stops her.*

Rainy   Mam, don't go. I'll go. Don't go like this. Don't spoil the day.

Cath   It's already spoiled, in't it?

Rainy   I'll find him. I'll go. Sit down. (*To* **Linda**.) You two aren't going. Don't let her go, Chris. (*To* **Cath**.) Just sit down, Mam.

Cath *sits on the bench.*

(*To* **Linda**.) It's not her against you 'cos you've taken him. You know it's not. Jesus, it might be a bloody sight easier to live with if it was. There was nobody more pleased when he first brought you home. Never stopped telling folk what a smashing lass you were, how you were the one. Still would be if all this business ant started up.

Linda   Yea, well 'this business' has nowt to do wi' me.

Cath   Your family.

Linda (*the present*)   And this is my family?

Cath   We know where your sympathies lie, lass, you can't be blamed for that.

Linda   Well you're wrong, and if you think I've turned his head against you, you're even more wrong. I wouldn't. I couldn't anyway. He makes his own mind up about things. He asked ME to live with HIM, or didn't he tell you that?

Cath   Turned against his own father.

Chris   I never turned against him. I thought he were wrong from 'start.

Cath   Oh, aye.

Chris   Yes, 'aye'. You know I did. I thought he were wrong and I said it.

Cath   Aye, and after you thought you'd proved your point, you kept rubbing it in.

Chris   I thought it were wrong of him to start filling in Mortal Ash, and I still do. Once that accident happened I tried to keep my mouth shut, he was the one kept bringing it all up. What happened made no difference to how I felt.

Cath   It should have.

Chris   Why?

Cath   If you don't know why, I'm not telling you.

Chris   It were an accident. It weren't summat brought down on his head like a bloody curse for interfering wi' nature, for God's sake.

Cath   That's what you made it seem like, lad.

Chris   How could I take back what was said?

Cath   You'll never know what you've done to him.

Chris   I'm a bad lot. 'Course, Eric's nowt to do with it and 'sun shines out of Duane's arse, he can do no wrong.

Cath   You've all given me your fair share of trouble, don't you worry, one time or another.

Rainy   Thanks.

Cath   What's he have to do a bloody daft trick like that for? How many times do I have to tell him to keep out of trouble? On his bloody birthday 'n all. You think 'day might come when you don't have to worry about your kids any more. Some hope. Nowt but trouble from day one, bloody lot of you. If I knew then what I know now –

Chris You'd 'ave never 'ave 'ad kids. Never 'ave got married. What would you have done, then, stayed at home and given your parents grief?

Cath That's one thing I never did.

Chris Yea, well, we can't all be perfect.

Cath I wish they were here now, I know that. There isn't a day goes by I don't miss 'em. Bless 'em. I wish they were here now to talk to. (*Pause.* **Cath** *is close to tears.*)

Rainy I'm going, Mam. I'll find him. Stop getting yourself in a state. It'll be all right.

She goes off. Pause.

Chris You were allus telling me I were the one who took after grandad.

Cath You do. He were tight as a duck's arse, an all. And stubborn. You're like him for that. Once you decide something . . . he were just the same.

Chris Is that a bad thing?

Cath Yes, when it's pride won't shift you. When it's your so-called principles that make you cut off your nose to spite your face. Not two 'apennies to rub together between you, over that flat, but you had to do what YOU wanted.

Chris Yea, well, it's hereditary, innit?

Cath It'll be God help yours if he turns out like you. (*To* **Linda**.) You wait and see. You think being together is a bed of roses. Aye, it might be till kids come along.

Linda That's why you had four, is it?

Cath Four kids, cats, dogs, canaries, lame bloody wildlife. I've nursed the lot. There's enough dead animals under here to grow bloody leeks ten foot tall. Next time around I'm coming back as a dog. That'd be the life. Or a man. Allus seem to get their own way. Your grandad used to say he wanted to come back as a Muslim. That way he could have four wives. One to wash and clean, one to cook, one to take out, and one to take to bed.

Chris A man after me own heart. (*To* **Linda**.) What? It were a joke.

Cath Just my luck to come back as a Muslim's wife.

Chris Which one?

Cath Bloody cook knowing me. (*Pause.*) It were your grandad made this. (*The bench.*) Him and your dad used to sit out here putting the world to rights. Didn't they? Sit for hours watching them birds. In their own world. Time meant nowt to 'em.

Chris Not after he lost his watch.

Cath Aye.

Chris (*to* **Linda**) We all went frogspawn collecting down the pond and he lost his watch. We never found it. I used to see him down there sometimes, sat on 'bank, looking out over 'water, and I'd say 'What you doing, Grandad?' and he'd say, 'I'm just looking to see what time it is'.

Pause. **Cath** *is crying.*

Cath Chris?

Chris What?

Cath Go down to 'pond and find him for me. Go on, all of you if you want. I'll be all right. Only ... come back, eh? (*Pause.*) Some bloody birthday. (*Pause.*) I'm a bloody evil old witch, aren't I?

Chris Yes.

Cath Out of my mouth before I can stop it. Way I'm going, I'm gunna finish up driving the lot of you away. Frightened of losing what I know I can't keep, that's what it is. Nowt can ever stay how you want it to stay, can it?

Linda No.

Cath Folk change. Place you live changes. When we were kids, paradise were at end of street. A couple of fields and you were there. Look at it all now. I don't know. I think what it is, it's not the place changing that hurts, it's yourself, when you see things going and they set you thinking about who you were, the way things used to be. Town's not what it was. Makes you sad because ... well, it's like that street's where 'picture house was, where I sat on the back row ... and don't any more. Nowt ever stays the same.

Linda No.

Cath When you're young, you want change. Want things to be modern, move on.

Chris I don't.

Cath No, because things now are changing too fast. We wanted progress then, a better life. When your dad were your age, he were union mad. But you see, all that's gone now. Everybody out for themselves. Gimme this. Gimme that. I want this, I want that. I don't know. When I were a little lass, all I ever wanted were long curly hair. Give my mother hell over that. I wanted hair like Lesley Tong and she wanted hair like mine. She got her wish one day.

Linda How?

Cath We were doing a plasticine nativity and I put a great dollop all in 'er 'air. Her mam had to cut it all out. I was a sod.

Linda I bet you were popular.

Cath I was. Anybody dared me to do owt and I'd do it. You ask his dad.

Linda You've known him since school?

Cath Since I were nine years old. Fourteen when I knew I wanted to marry him. Summat about him. He were a little gentleman. They had an allotment just up from ours. I used to take chicken mash up in a bucket on a Sunday

morning, and watch him. He'd go blood red whenever he
caught me looking. Then he got to timing it so we'd both
get to 'communal tap at 'same time and he'd carry me
bucket o' water back for me.

Chris Very romantic.

Cath He was. Bought me a bottle of 'Evening Primrose'
perfume off 'market wi' 'is first wages. Said I smelled like
Mortal Ash on a summer's night.

Chris Should 'ave saved his money and just got you
rolling about a bit.

Cath Your dad weren't like that.

Chris Eh? I meant rolling down the hill.

Cath I know what you meant. Used to be covered in
primroses up there. A carpet of them, when we were
young.

Chris Used to be horses and carts when she were young.

Cath I'm not that old. We had one or two about, still,
delivering coal and what have you. I used to have to go
out after he'd been, wi' a bucket and shovel. Made
'rhubarb grow a treat. Used to like a stick o' rhubarb. Dip
it in 'sugar bowl.

Chris Grow some, then, you've got space now.

Cath Aye.

Chris Duane'll collect the 'oss shit.

Cath Plenty of bonemeal down 'ere.

Chris So do it, then.

Cath We ought to do summat wi' it. Looks a state like
this. Concrete the bugger.

Chris We used to have a bit of veg growing one time.

Cath We did, but wi' four of you traipsing in and out,
digging holes, treading on stuff . . .

Chris   Rainy had her own garden. Dad give her a square somewhere. Planted some seeds.

Cath   What did it were that day me and your dad went to town, came back and you'd all built a den. Bloody hole that big, there were about ten kids in it.

Chris   We covered it up.

Cath   Aye, you did. Got some corrugated sheets from somewhere. When your dad lifted it up, they were all sat wi' torches and a knicker page each out me catalogue.

They laugh.

I'll tell you, Linda, if and when you two do decide to have kids, make sure you live in a house with about three acres. It'll still look like No Man's Land if you have lads.

Linda   Which would you like?

Cath   Eh?

Linda   Grandson or grandaughter.

Cath   Wouldn't bother me, lass, as long as they were healthy. Anyway, you don't want to be thinking about that till you've got some money behind you. 'Cos if you've got nowt when you start wi' a family, you sure as hell won't have when you do. You're not, are you?

Linda   What?

Cath   Thinking about it? Not while you're still in that rabbit hutch anyroad.

Chris   We'll get off wi' Rainy, eh? In case there's any trouble. Best go down.

Cath   Aye, if you want.

Chris   We'll come back.

Cath   I've done plenty. Your dad'll be in soon.

Chris   We won't be long.

Cath   I'd better put water on, he'll be wanting a bath

when he gets in. (*She gets up, takes the present from* **Linda**.) It'll be melting. I'll put it in 'fridge. (*She goes in.*)

Linda *looks at* **Chris**.

Chris   Yea, all right.

Linda   I never said a word.

They go off.

Scene Three

The kitchen, half an hour later. **Duane** *is naked but for his underpants, almost completely covered in calamine lotion.* **Cath** *is dabbing it on his body with cotton wool.* **Rainy**, **Chris** *and* **Linda** *look on.*

Duane (*chattering and sucking through his teeth*)   I had to get the fishing rod back out, din't I? When I waded in, they chucked me clothes in after me an' all. I were sinking in sinking mud, like quicksand. I cunt find it. They were laughing, and when I come back out they just got hold of me. Picked me up, carried me over to 'nettles. I cunt do owt. They just swung me up and over. One. Two. I din't think they would. Three. Let go. I just went flying.

Rainy   You look like a zombie.

Duane   A what?

Rainy   One of them dead people that come alive.

Duane (*pleased*)   Do I? (*He does a little* Thriller *dance.*)

Cath   Stand still.

Duane   It kills. It's cold that stuff.

Cath   Do you want to be itching all night?

Duane   No.

Cath   Well, then. Stand still. (*To* **Rainy**.) You'll have to get me another bottle of calamine. I've nearly used this lot.

Duane   Am I gunna have to wear pyjamas?

Cath   Yes.

Duane   We could have a pyjama party.

Cath   You don't deserve any party.

Duane   Why not?

Cath   You should have bloody well left alone this morning. I've told you often enough.

Duane   You dint 'ear 'em.

Cath   What was said?

Duane   They were saying stuff and that.

Cath   What stuff?

Duane   About dad and Eric and that.

Rainy   Duane.

Cath   Duane, I want you to promise me –

Duane   They started chucking bricks first!

Cath   Listen! You walk away, do you hear? You walk away.

Duane   I'm supposed to do nowt when they say stuff?

Cath   Yes.

Duane   I'd 'ave bloody smacked 'em if I'd got 'old of 'em. All of 'em.

Cath   Aye, and you'd 'ave finished up worse than this.

Duane   I don't give a toss.

Cath   What's the matter with you? Are you totally senseless or what?

Chris   Yes.

Duane   Get stuffed.

Cath   Well you're acting like it. You're gunna finish up putting me in an early grave at this rate. We give 'em nowt to stir things up. Do you hear me?

Duane   Yes.

Cath   Well, then. I want no more. Promise me.

Duane   Yea, all right.

Cath   Say it.

Duane   I've said it.

Cath   Duane.

Duane   I promise. All right? I'll walk away. I'll be a coward if that's what you want.

Chris   It's not being a coward. Fighting's easy. Walking away from it all is what takes the guts.

Duane   Like you, you mean?

Cath   That'll do. That's enough. Just think on, my lad, that's all I'm asking. Just use your head. I want you to promise me summat else 'n all.

Duane   What?

Cath   Promise me you won't go down to that place any more.

Duane   Mortal Ash?

Cath   Yes.

Duane   I'm not. You get disease.

Cath   You what?

Duane   Summatitis.

Cath   What you on about?

Duane   Does your brain in. It swells up and bursts.

Rainy   Shut up, Duane.

Duane   What?

Cath What?

Rainy Him going on.

Duane What is it? Summatitis. Somebody's got it. You get it from rat piss. If you cut yourself and get rat piss in it, you get this disease. Some kid's got it.

Cath (*to* **Rainy**) What's he on about?

Rainy I don't know.

Duane Well I ant got it.

Chris You ant got no brain to get diseased.

Duane Sod off.

Cath Well keep away. Do you hear?

Duane Yes.

Cath I'll get your pyjamas. (*To* **Rainy**.) Did I put water on?

Rainy I put it on.

Cath (*to* **Duane**) And don't, for God's sake, say owt to your dad when he gets in.

Duane As if.

Cath I know you. Tell him you fell. (*She goes off.*)

Chris (*to* **Duane**) you stupid get.

Duane What have I done?

Rainy I didn't want her to know about it.

Duane What?

Rainy Who told you?

Duane What about?

Rainy Who?

Duane Them kids this morning.

Linda What is it?

Rainy There were a big article in 'Gazette. I read it on 'bus and binned it when I got off.

Linda What did it say?

Rainy There's two kids in 'infirmary wi' suspected meningitis.

Duane That's it.

Rainy They reckon there might be a link wi' Mortal Ash. Kids going on 'tip.

Linda I can't see ... I mean surely nobody's going to make anything of it?

Rainy No?

Linda It's the council what's tipping.

Chris It's everybody what's tipping. But dad and Eric cleared the site, started draining 'ponds for Hicks. That's all folk see. They were the ones down there when all 'protesting started.

Linda If it had'nt been them it would have been somebody else.

Rainy But it wasn't.

Linda How can your dad be blamed for some kids playing on a tip, when they shouldn't be there anyway? It's like saying if you 'adn't 'a built 'Umber Bridge, there'd be people alive now who didn't chuck themselves off it. It's daft. If you're gunna do it, you do it. If kids are gunna play in filth, they're gunna find it wherever.

Rainy You said yourself what's happening round 'ere. Mob rule dunt go by logic.

Pause. **Duane** *examines his spots.*

Chris If he'd 'ave done what I said, walked off after 'accident.

Rainy I don't want to know.

Chris Every day he went to work he were making it worse.

Rainy Is that what you told him?

Chris Wasn't he? Bloody Hicks never comes near, but dad had to keep working. Like it never meant owt when she –

Linda Chris. Don't.

Chris If he'd 'ave done what I said, none of this would have happened.

Rainy You do blame him. You bloody well –

Chris I don't blame him. I'm not saying that. I never said I thought Eric or dad were to blame for owt, other than bulldozing 'place when it shunt 'a been.

Rainy No wonder he feels the way he docs. You going on at him.

Chris It's his conscience, not my saying owt.

Duane *traces a line of spots on his stomach.*

How were I to know what would happen? How did I know it were guuna come to all this? Don't you pin this on me. He thinks and does what he wants. What I've said's gone in one ear and out of 'other. I'm not responsible for what's going on in his head.

Rainy You're his son!

Pause.

Duane Have we got a biro?

Rainy What for?

Duane I want to join up the dots. There's an 'orse 'ere. Or it's a bloke wi' 'is 'ead up another bloke's arse.

Rainy Is that dry?

Duane Yea.

Rainy   Go and put some pyjamas on, then.

Duane   She's bringing 'em.

Chris   Prat.

Duane   Up yours. (*He makes to go off.*)

Rainy   Where you going now?

Duane   I'm off for a piss, all right? (*He goes off.*)

Chris (*to* **Rainy**)   So I'm not entitled to an opinion, then?

Rainy *ignores him. He looks at* **Linda**.

Linda   There's a time and a place, Chris.

Chris   You what? Oh, great.

Linda   I don't understand how you can say all you've said to him, fight him, but your mam —

Chris   What?

Linda   Why are you so scared to upset her?

Chris   What do you mean?

Linda   You know what I mean.

Chris   No I don't.

Linda   Tell her and be done with it. About the baby. And if she says owt, well at least you've told her. It's not my job.

Chris   I'm gunna tell her.

Linda   When? She needs summat out of all this. It can only go one way or 'other, Chris, whenever you tell her. (*Pause. To* **Rainy**.) We're giving him your dad's middle name as his middle name.

Rainy   Verdun.

Linda   Yes. Whether it's a boy or a girl.

Rainy   That's nice. She'll like that. What about 'first name?

Linda We ant thought, yet.

Rainy You know where it comes from?

Linda Your grandad.

Rainy Yes. That's where his dad were killed in 'First World War. Somewhere abroad. Never saw his son, so they called him Verdun.

Chris *moves off, goes through.*

Linda I think it's in France.

Rainy Yea.

Linda I'd like to go abroad.

Rainy Yea. I nearly got there.

Linda Him at work.

Rainy Got my passport anyway.

Linda Didn't you say you might be off next year?

Rainy I'm supposed to be off to Greece wi'a couple of lasses from work. They went in July. Said it were brilliant.

Linda It'll be good.

Rainy I hope so. I'm having second thoughts.

Linda You want to go, you'll have a good time.

Rainy Yea.

Linda You will. You can't be here all 'time, can you?

Rainy No. They come back with a brilliant tan. All over.

Linda They never.

Rainy They did.

Linda I cunt do that.

Rainy No, me neither. I don't go brown anyway, just lobster. I hope it's not too hot. They were dropping like flies out there the other year.

Linda I've got some of that Hawaii Five O if you want to borrow it.

Rainy I bought some Ambrie Solaire.

Linda Stop you getting burnt.

Rainy They met two bricklayers from Sunderland.

Linda Oh, aye? Sounds very Mills and Boon.

Rainy Had a good time.

Linda Yea, well, be sensible.

Rainy Yea, I suppose.

They have a dirty laugh together. **Tom** *comes into the yard, carrying his case.* **Linda** *sees him.*

Linda There's your dad here.

Tom *comes into the kitchen.*

Rainy Hiya.

Tom Now, then. Hello, Linda.

Linda Hello.

Tom Chris here?

Rainy He's with mam.

Tom Where is she?

Rainy Upstairs I think.

Tom (*shouting off*) Anybody in? (*To* **Rainy**.) I could do wi' a cup o' tea.

Rainy *starts to make him one. He puts his case down, takes out the Gazette from his pocket, puts it on the table, sits.*

I'm worn out. (*He takes a sausage roll, begins to eat it.*)

Rainy I'll bet you are.

Tom Where's birthday boy, then?

Rainy Upstairs.

Tom   What's he think of 'present?

Rainy   Mam hasn't given it to him yet. She wanted to wait for you.

Tom   Oh.

Rainy   He knows what it is.

Tom   Aye. Quizzing you all, I bet.

Linda   What is it?

Tom   Summat he'll appreciate, I hope. Over two hundred quid I've spent on him. (*Pause. Shouting, off.*)   I'm home! (*To* **Rainy**.) What they doing?

Rainy   Just talking. (*She comes to the table, sees the paper.*)

Tom (*to* **Linda**)   So how's things, then?

Linda   Fine. (*She catches* **Rainy**'s *eye.*)

Tom   You're all right?

Linda   Yes, thanks.

Tom   Good. Has he brought them brushes back?

Linda   I'm not ... no, I don't think so.

Tom   I'm only joking.

Rainy   You got a paper, then.

Tom   Gazette.

Rainy   Owt in it?

Tom   Shunt think so, never is. I ant read it yet. (*Looks at table.*)   Done enough, ant she? How many we expecting? Half of street, looks like.

Rainy   Just us lot.

Tom (*to* **Linda**)   Allus makes a spread on birthdays. (*To* **Rainy**.)   Likes to do summat a bit special, dun't she?

Rainy   Yes.

Tom   It's daft, now you've all grown up, but it's summat she's allus done. Makes her happy.

Rainy   Makes us happy. I like it.

Tom   Aye. Lets her think you're still kids again.

Rainy   It gets us together.

Tom (*to* **Linda**)   Used to have half of 'kids in street round one time. All went home wi' a balloon and a lucky dip.

Duane *comes in, dressed in his pyjamas. Face white with calamine.*

Duane   All right?

Tom   What the hell's up wi' you?

Duane   Nowt. I fell in some nettles.

Tom   I thought she'd gone and booked Coco the Clown.

Duane   Give over.

Tom   What do you look like?

Duane   Michael Jackson.

Tom   Aye, on a good day. Happy birthday, anyroad.

Duane   Thanks, Dad.

Tom   How many cards you got?

Chris *and* **Cath** *come in.*

Cath   You're here, then.

Tom   I see you've been busy.

Cath   It's only a bit.

Tom   Enough to feed five thousand.

Cath   There isn't.

Tom (*to* **Chris**)   Where's beard, then?

Chris   I shaved it off.

Duane Give up trying to grow it, you mean.

Chris No.

Duane Linda blew him a kiss and it all flew off.

They laugh.

Chris Give over.

Duane Bum fluff.

Tom When did you shave it off?

Chris About a month ago.

Linda It made me itch.

Cath (*to* **Tom**) It were a better beard than you ever managed.

Chris Did you have a beard?

Cath Before we were married. Hair down his back, all this round here. Looked like a bloody yeti.

Tom Give over.

Cath Had one of them shaggy dog coats.

Tom Afghan.

Linda Were you a hippy, then?

Tom Me?

Cath He lived in that coat. It were lousy. Stunk of yak shit an 'all. I'm sure when he took it off it used to crawl by itself to 'ook at back of their kitchen door. He thought he looked the bee's knees in it.

Chris Did you wear beads an' all that?

Tom Did I buggery.

Chris I bet you did. I bet you looked a right soft get.

Tom I weren't a bloody hippy. I had my own style, me. My own man, went me own way. Bloody nancy's them lot.

Rainy (*to* **Cath**)   Were you an 'ippy, then?

Cath   Aye. (*To* **Tom**.) I got converted under a sleeping bag in Jubilee park. Di 'nt I?

Tom (*embarrassed*)   Aye, all right.

Pause.

Cath   Right, then. (*To* **Chris**.) Shall you tell him or shall I?

Chris *shrugs, embarrassed.*

Tom   What?

Cath   You're going to be a grandad.

Tom (*looking at* **Chris**)   Eh?

Cath   Her, you silly bugger. Linda.

Tom   Oh. You're having a baby, then?

They laugh.

Cath   What do you think she's having? (*To* **Linda**.) Come 'ere. Come on.

Linda *goes to her.* **Cath** *hugs her.*

Congratulations, love.

Linda   Thank you.

Cath (*to* **Tom**)   Well?

Tom   Aye. Congratulations.

Duane   Uncle Duane. Bloody hell.

Cath   I knew.

Chris   You didn't.

Cath   I knew, I'm telling you.

Chris   How?

Cath   Mothers know.

Tom   Well it's lovely. I'm . . .

Cath   In't it lovely?

Tom   Aye. Champion. I'm well pleased for 'pair of you.

Cath   Double celebration now, eh?

Duane   When am I getting me present?

Cath   What present?

Duane   Ant you got me owt?

Cath goes to cupboard, brings out a tiny wrapped box, hands it to him.

Is this it?

Cath   Yes.

Duane   No wonder I cunt find it. (*He opens it. Takes out the shed key.*) A key?

Cath   You're the one been playing detective. Come on.

Pause.

Duane   Oh.

He goes out to the shed, the others following, **Rainy** *last, picking up the newspaper as she goes. They watch him go in and bring out all his new fishing tackle — box, rods, holdalls, etc.*

Brilliant. Oh, thanks. Brilliant.

Cath   You like it, then?

Duane   It's brilliant.

Cath   Bring it in, then, take it through. You've got all sorts in that box an' all.

Tom   No excuse for not catching owt now, eh?

Duane   No.

Tom   You'll have to come wi' me.

Duane   Yea.

Duane *takes his tackle in, followed by* **Tom** *and* **Cath**.

Chris   Who's gunna tell him his gear's at bottom of Mortal Ash?

Rainy   Shut it, Chris. (*She puts the newspaper in the dustbin. Goes in.*)

In the kitchen.

Tom   What else you got?

Duane   Floats, tape, fruit and nut.

Cath   I've had water on, ready for your bath.

Tom   Aye, right. I stink a bit.

Cath   And when you come down, it'll all be ready. (*She goes through with* **Duane**.)

Tom   Cup o' tea.

Rainy   I'll bring it up.

Tom   Where's paper?

Rainy   I thought you'd read it.

Tom   No. What you done wi' it?

Rainy *goes out, gets the paper from the bin, comes in again, gives it to him.*

Tom   Don't know whether you're coming or going, do you? Aunty Lorraine. You next.

Rainy   You've got to be joking.

He goes off. **Rainy** *pours the kettle into the pot.*

In the yard.

Linda   Thanks, Chris.

Pause. We hear music off – Def Leppard from **Duane**'s *cassette player.*

In the kitchen. **Cath** *comes in.*

Cath   Shall we 'ave cloth on 'table?

Rainy   No, we're all right.

Cath   Yes, do it proper. Make it look nice.

Rainy   Where is it?

Cath   I can do it. Go upstairs and see if you can find me them plastic doilies. They're in 'tallboy in our bedroom. Better take Linda with you, I don't want it falling on top of you when you pull 'drawers out, looking.

Rainy *goes out to the yard. Stops. Watches* **Chris** *and* **Linda**. **Cath** *hums to herself as she takes out the cloth, spreads it.*

Rainy   Linda? Give us 'and a minute.

Linda *goes in, follows* **Rainy** *through.* **Chris** *comes into the kitchen.*

Cath   I told you he'd be pleased.

Chris   Yea.

Cath   Best news we could have wished for. Your grandad would have been so proud. (*Pause. She sets out seven places at the table.*)

Chris   How many of us is there? There's only six.

Cath   That's Eric's place.

Chris   Eh?

Cath   I know. I just want to do it. All right?

Chris   You're mad.

Cath   So I've been told. (*He goes through. She hums to herself.*)

Act Two

Scene One

The yard. After the party. **Tom** *is sat on the bench having a fag, reading the paper.* **Cath** *is in the kitchen, clearing up. She comes out to shake the table cloth.* **Tom** *puts down the paper.*

Cath Did you enjoy your tea?

Tom Yes, you've worked hard.

Cath Lovely to have everybody here.

Tom Aye.

Pause.

Cath It feels funny knowing we're going to be grandparents. Don't you think?

Tom How do you mean?

Cath I don't know. Don't you think it does?

Tom I suppose it does.

Pause.

Cath I think they mean to make a go of it.

Tom Bloody better do now.

Cath I mean ... I think ... well, it's what they want. They seem happy enough.

Tom Are they getting married?

Cath I think she wants to. I think they will one day. (*Pause.*) Verdun. I think that's lovely to do that. Don't you?

Tom Long as it's healthy.

Cath Yes. Don't seem five minutes since he was crawling about out here. Picking up anything to put in his mouth. Do you remember?

Tom Yes.

Cath Ants. Beetles. All went in his mouth. That little pedal car he had. (*Pause.*) I hope they're going to manage.

Tom They will or they won't.

Cath They've not got much between 'em. (*Pause.*) He's back on basic now.

Tom Is he?

Cath Linda says they might be laying them off. That or on a three day week.

Tom Well there's nowt round here now.

Cath No. (*Pause.*) I, er . . . I said we'd help 'em out. (*Pause.*) Baby clothes and that.

Tom Oh, aye?

Cath Well we've got his money for him, haven't we?

Tom Good idea.

Cath It'd get push-chair and what have you.

Tom Yes. You told him, then?

Cath Well I were talking to Linda.

Tom What's she say?

Cath Well she'd appreciate it.

Tom What's he say?

Cath Well he will.

Tom You told him?

Cath No, not yet. (*Pause.*)

Tom What?

Cath Nothing. (*Pause.*) I said I'd let Linda have it when she needed it.

Tom Why? (*Pause.*) You think he won't tek it?

Cath Course he'll tek it.

Tom Well, then?

Cath He's just . . . Well you know what a funny bugger he is. I don't want . . . I'd rather do it like this.

Tom Either he teks it out me 'and or he dunt 'ave it.

Cath Don't be daft. You don't have to do it like that.

Tom I'm not ashamed of where it came from. Are you?

Cath No.

Tom So why give it to 'em on 'sly? If he can't tek it up front he can do wi'out.

Cath It's just . . . you know how he feels about it.

Tom About what? (*Pause.*) Sod him. I'll know where I stand, then, won't I? (*Pause.*) Do you really think he wouldn't tek it? (*Pause.*) Well he can do without, then. I'll share it out wi' rest. They're happy to take what we've given 'em. They're all right. It's just that bugger.

Pause.

Cath If that's what you'd rather do. (*Pause.*) What do I say to Linda?

Tom You shunt 'ave offered it her. What's bloody point of 'em having it, if he dunt know where it's come from?

Cath Does he have to know?

Tom 'Course he does.

Cath Why? Do you want him to thank you for it? Do you want him to be grateful?

Tom I don't want nowt from him.

Cath Well, then. A gift is a gift. You give 'cos you want to, not to be thanked for it.

Tom That's not point. You're saying he won't 'ave owt to do wi' it if he knows where it comes from. Either the bloody money's honest or it in't. In't it? In't it honest?

Cath   Yes.

Tom   Get him out 'ere.

Cath   I don't think –

Tom   Let's find out one way or 'other.

Cath   You'll only finish up –

Tom   I don't give a sod! I want this thing sorted once and for all. I mean it.

Cath   You want him, you fetch him.

Pause. **Tom** *gets up, goes into the kitchen, shouts through.*

Tom   Chris?!

Chris (*off*)   What?

Tom   Here. Here a minute. (**Tom** *comes back into the yard. Waits. To* **Cath**.) Go on, then.

Cath   I'm staying 'ere.

Tom   We don't need a referee.

Chris *comes through and out.*

Chris   What?

Cath   We've been thinking about you and Linda and 'baby. We know you're short, so we thought we might help you out with a few essentials.

Pause.

Chris   Thanks. That's good of you.

Cath   You'll let us?

Chris   Well we're gunna need stuff, I suppose. Thanks. Thanks, Dad.

Pause.

Tom   So I'll give you 'money next week, when I've been

to 'bank.

Chris   Next week? We've got eight month yet. Get bits when you can.

Tom   I want you to have 'money. That road you can get what you want when you want.

Chris   OK.

Tom   Everybody else has had a share ... Duane's gear, Rainy for her 'oliday ... and Eric's getting his when ... you've all got two hundred and fifty pound.

Pause.

Chris   A share? Of what?

Cath   Money we've been saving.

Chris   Oh.

Tom   Money I earnt as bonus. From Hicks.

Pause.

Chris   What are you saying?

Tom   What do you think I'm saying?

Chris   What do you – (*Pause*) Dad.

Tom   What?

Chris   Why do you have to ...? Why tell me where it's from?

Tom   You'd rather not know?

Chris   Yes. No. If you'd just given me –

Tom   You could 'a teken it. But now you can't.

Chris   How can I after what I've said? After all I've said to you? You know I can't. Don't – (*Pause.*) Dad.

Tom   Aye, well, we know now.

Chris   What?

Tom   What I am to you.

Chris   Don't be daft.

Tom   It's all right.

Chris   Dad, please.

Tom   Every bugger else thinks I'm a wrong 'un, why not you?

Cath   He doesn't think that.

Tom   In't it 'onest money, then?

Chris   I'm not getting into this.

Tom   Tek it, then!

Chris   I can't.

Tom   Well do wi'out the bloody money, then! (*Pause.*) Who do you think I did it for? My own sweat, my own labour. In't that honest enough? More bloody honest made than where most of it comes from, out of some bugger else's labour. Your bloody yuppies making a killing. Aye, they do. Principles? You're not telling me the bloody money market's run on principles. All for one and one for all. Bollocks. Everybody trying to climb up the ladder, knocking everybody else off. I've never in my life done that. Never. Every penny I've ever earnt, I earnt wi' these, for you lot. Well you can arseholes!

Pause.

Cath (*to* **Tom**)   Are you satisfied now? (*Pause.*) I don't want any more. I've had enough of all this. Away all week and you come back and start this. What kind of a week do you think I've had? He's been mending the window for me all morning that somebody smashed last night. He's been helping me.

Tom (*to* **Chris**)   What is it that's so bad about me, eh? What kind of a man do you really think I am? Eh? Come on, tell me. Such an evil bastard for getting rid of Mortal Ash. Eh?

Chris It's not that.

Tom What is it, then? Tell me. Come on, tell me.

Pause.

Chris Why you kept working after the accident. It's that.

Cath Oh, you bloody –

Chris That's what I can't understand.

Tom What you can't forgive, you mean.

Chris I might if you told me why you did it.

Cath Leave it. I told you to leave it!

Tom Do I 'ave to account for missen to you?

Cath No, you don't.

Chris You were always . . . Doesn't it matter to you what I think of what you did?

Tom Think what you want.

Chris I've told you what I think a thousand times but you . . . Why don't you defend yourself?

Cath He doesn't have to defend hisself to his own son.

Chris He does!

Tom No I bloody well don't! I answer to nobody but missen and him up there. Not to you, my lad, not to you. (*To* **Cath**.) And I don't need you defending me neither.

Cath I don't want no upset. Not today. (*To* **Chris**.) Stop it, do you hear?

Chris If I've got it wrong, you should tell me. That's all I want. If you won't say owt, what am I supposed to think? It's important to me, Dad. It's important. I don't want to be forever trying to figure it out, wondering who the hell me Dad was. I want to understand you.

Tom Aye, well, there's your first lesson in life.

Chris What?

Tom None of us know bugger all about anybody. And 'folks closest to you are 'biggest bloody mystery of all.

Cath Thank you.

Tom You know what I mean.

Cath Do I? I should hope I know you.

Tom I don't even know my bloody self, so you've got no chance.

Cath Can't we have some peace for one day?!

Tom Only peace I get is when I'm out this house.

Cath *turns away from them.*

You know what I mean! I don't mean ...

Cath You're determined to lose him, aren't you? (*She goes in. We see her sat in the kitchen, listening.*)

Chris So are you saying you don't know yourself why you did it?

Tom You'll know what I'm on about one day.

Chris I'm not a kid. I'm not wet behind the ears any more. Don't put me off with generation gap crap. Older and wiser.

Tom You think when you get to my age you have it all worked out? Understand it all? Have a reason for everything you do? Have all 'answers worked out? Older you get, more bloody fog rolls in.

Chris What are you saying, then? You telling me you don't know why you did it?

Tom You think I were never like you? Never had principles to live by? You think I've lived a life wi'out any causes to fight? I would have laid down my life for causes I believed in then. (*Pause.*) I can't even remember what they were now. (*Pause.*) Whatever they were, I know they were about summat more important than a few trees and a stagnant pond.

Chris   To me it was important.

Tom   Aye, well, you see, that's where we're allus gunna come unstuck, then, in't it?

Chris   It was important to you. I know what the place meant to you and I know you felt you had to keep working for the money. It's not that. It's why you kept working after the girl was killed. In the face of folks's fury, why?

Tom   Maybe that's why.

Chris   What? Defying them? You did it for that?

Tom   Maybe it were 'first principle I'd thought about in twenty years.

Chris   What principle?

Tom   Do what you have to do, and don't let other folks stop you.

Chris   'A man's gotta do . . .'

Tom   You what?

Chris   Nowt.

Tom   You take the piss out of me, lad, you'll know about it. (*Pause.*) In't it important to do what you think is right?

Chris   You thought it right?

Tom   Yes.

Chris   How? How was it right?

Tom   You think they were right? To come on to private land?

Chris   Everybody uses –

Tom   Trying to stop a bloke from doing his work, what he's told to do? What he tries to do wi'out interfering wi' anybody?

Chris They have a right to protest.

Tom Aye, same way as they're protesting now. Filling the
place wi' their own rubbish. It were just summat for 'em to
do. Summat a bit exciting. Chuck bricks at us. Run in
front o' bulldozer. You think they were doing it out o'
principles? What bloody principles do folk round here live
by? Eh? Look after your own and bugger anybody else.

Chris And you're different? Weren't that what you were
doing?

Tom I were working. I were doing a job. It's gunna keep
other folks in work when they build 'place – them that
wants it. Most of them buggers coming on that site, they
don't know what work is. Don't bloody want it. Stand on
'street corners bored out of their minds till some'dy tells
'em what I'm up to, so they think 'Let's go and chuck a
few bricks at Tom Wheatley. Summat to do. Bit of a
laugh.'

Chris You think they want to be out of work?

Tom Some of 'em 's made a bloody career out of it.

Chris But those that want to –

Tom So they take it out on me? 'Cause I'm working and
they're not? (*Pause.*)

Chris Dad. A girl was killed. We're talking about after
that. After, it's about work? (*Pause.*) Didn't you feel you
should have stopped? For her? Out of respect for her?

Tom You mean like City of London stops after a bomb's
gone off, killed half a dozen? Tomorrow's just another
working day.

Chris That's not the same. That's about defying
terrorists, in't it?

Tom Defiance my arse, it's about not wanting to stop
making money.

Chris   And you? (*Pause.*) Didn't it occur to you it might get nasty? Didn't it dawn on you what might happen? Couldn't you have waited until the inquest at least? I know enough about you, Dad, to know you care about summat else. All you've said, you still care about people. Hate 'em, yes, but ... I've seen you when 'news is on. I've seen tears in your eyes for what's going on in 'world. People still matter, even when they're not your own. Even more when it's a young life. So why? (*Pause.*) Tell me! Tell me it weren't just about money!

Tom   You think you know why I get up every day and go to work, same thing day after day, year in year out? (*Pause.*) Summat more than money, lad.

Chris   What?

Tom   I used to wonder why some blokes get to retirement and six months yon side of it they're six foot under.

Chris   Why?

Tom   Because first chance they get to look at themselves, they can't abide what they see. Worry themselves to death trying to figure it out. Look in a mirror and you don't know who the hell it is. Look out the window and you don't bloody recognize any of it for what it really is. Frightens 'em to death.

Chris   What are you saying?

Tom   You keep going. If you stop work, you start thinking, and fog rolls in. You hate work but you hate not to more, because you've worked all your life and known nowt else and 'prospect of stopping is ... when have you ever know me to have a day off work?

Chris   You ant.

Tom   Saving it all up for when I pack in.

Chris   That's stupid.

Tom   Course it is. That's just 'point. It's stupid, it makes no sense. That's what fear is, in't it?

Chris   Fear? You were never frightened in your life.

Tom   Aye, well there's 'second lesson in life. You're doing well today.

Chris   Eh?

Tom   When I were your age, maybe I were frightened of nobody. Fought the bastards till we got what we wanted. Then what happened? How do you think I felt, no work, bloody union beaten to death, having to go cap in 'and? Bloody yes sir, no sir, three bags full sir, to bring a wage home at 'end of 'week? Brought to your bloody knees and made to either do what they want you to do for a bloody pittance, or get out altogether. Felt like bloody inquisition, or summat. Yes, I was a union man, sir, I confess my sins, but I've seen the error of my ways and won't cause you no trouble no more. And I haven't. Kept at it. Kept me 'ead down, just got on wi' it like I were told to, otherwise I'd a bin out, that'd a bin it. No job.
It weighs on you more than money, more than responsibility to 'bloke who pays your wages. You're weighed down wi' doing it, 'cause you don't want to think about not doing it. And either you carry the bloody weight like ballast, getting shot of it at sixty-five and keel over, or use the bugger to heave yourself into 'river.
I don't give a toss about what folk say and think I did. I made me own peace wi' lass my own way. It dunt 'ave to be public, parading me feelings in 'street, like some buggers do, making 'em feel they've done the right thing – more folk see 'em crying, better they feel about it. I don't need anybody to hear me say how sorry I am. I know. And if she can hear me, wherever she is, she knows. I don't need you to know, Chris, your mam nor nobody. You see in me what you want to see. If folk think I should make my respect public or suffer them getting at us the way they have . . . if they're right and I'm wrong . . . if you're telling me what they've done is right and what I've done is wrong . . .

Chris   I'm not.

Tom   You are.

Chris   I wanted it explaining, that's all.

Tom   You said you didn't want to go on thinking bad of me all your life. At 'end of day, you're still wanting to judge me. Was I wrong?

Chris   You said it didn't matter what I thought.

Tom   It oughtn't. But it does. (*Pause.*) Well? (*Pause.*)

Chris   I can't see it. (*Pause.*) I'm sorry. I just . . .

Tom   So my money's not 'onest earnt, then. Eh? (*Pause.*) Any of it?

Chris   You think it is.

Tom   You! You!

Chris   It doesn't matter what I –

Tom   It is or it isn't. Right or wrong. Not what I think, not what you think.

Chris   But you said –

Tom   Tell me! Somebody bloody tell me! (*Pause.*) If it's wrong . . . All of it'll go back in 'pond. I'll tek the lot, bloody fishing tackle, bloody holiday clothes and what have you, I'll chuck the bloody lot in. Will that satisfy you?

Chris   Will it satisfy you?

Tom   Aye, p'raps it might at that.

Chris   Don't do it for me.

Tom   I am doing it for you. Who else?

Chris   For you!

Tom   I don't fucking know who me is, except through you. Can't you see that?! (*Pause.*) You're all I can keep in 'ere. Owt else just finishes up mush as soon as I start to think about it. What you are, what you might become.

That's it. (*Pause.*) If I can't square this with you . . .

Chris What's this? Last will and testament? You sound
like you're about to peg it.

Tom Only thing you can be certain's going to 'appen.
(*Pause.*) What's 'point of planning owt, but somehow
through you? You can't plan owt else in life wi' any
certainty it'll 'appen. Apart from having a bowl of All-Bran
for breakfast, being sure of a good shit.
Everything's on shifting sand. Nowt for sure. That's
progress, in't it?
I don't know. All I know is 'world seems to be turning
faster; you have all on hanging on to the bugger. Issue
everybody wi' lead boots.
You're all I am, Chris. 'Cause you were 'first, I suppose.
Not favourite. We never had favourites. You know that.

Chris I know.

Tom All of you's important to me. But even wi' it
seeming like you're furthest away . . . from whatever I am
. . . and you are, no getting away from that . . . we're not
close, we're not close wi' all this . . . talking . . . showing
feelings. That's not you, not your fault, that's me, that's
way I am, made you the way you are wi' us. Summat
went haywire somewhere . . . I mean, I stopped feeling owt
for me own. Buried it. Aye. Filled it all in wi' rubbish.
Yes, I can feel summat for somebody thousands of miles
away on 'telly. My . . . my heart breaks wi' summat.
Summat for 'em. I don't understand it. They're suffering,
and I'm a cold stone in my own backyard. I do care, I do.
Your mam. You lot. Other folk, even. But it's so far down
and covered in crap. (*Pause.*)

Chris We know you care. Even if you can't show it. It's
just understood. Mam knows. Yea, you row about stuff, I
row with her about stuff, but you do it because . . . I know
why you work away all week, I know part of it's . . . well,
when you're together you talk to one another like you're
just making up conversation to fill in time . . . but things
don't have to be said.

Tom Aye, till one day it's too late to say what you've wanted to say for years. They do, Chris, they do have to be said, but . . . why is it so hard to speak what's in 'ere? What is it keeps me blinkered and lead booted?
I were like you. I were. World meant summat. There was summat else. But your ideals disappear, like your friends. I were in control, then. Stuff going on in 'world. Confident. Cocksure. Whatever 'appened, you rode it all. Like you were on a bloody surfboard, if you fell off, you just got on again. Traded it all in along the way for comfort. Safety. Did I? Is that what happened? What the fuck happened? Close down the hatches. Sit in the dark. On your own. Together. Sow your seed. You're 'only part of me that's out there in the sun.

Pause. **Catherine**, *in the kitchen, is crying. She holds her hand over her mouth to stop the cry coming out.*

I have to square this with you. I can't work it out on my own. Tell me what I should do. Don't chuck it back at me . . . I've nowt to work it out with. Just tell me and I'll do what you want. (*Pause.*) My own . . . (*He covers his eyes.*) couldn't see. Is that what's caused all this? (*Pause.*) She wouldn't have died.

Chris It was an accident.

Tom I told him to keep working. Keep tipping. If they wanted to play dare down bottom of 'banking, run out of 'way when he tipped it all, their look out. Couldn't get out of the way. Caught her sandal. Buried her in breezeblocks.

Chris You can't keep thinking –

Tom Blind to folks's feelings. But I wouldn't listen. Couldn't. Not even to your mam.

(*Pause.*)

Chris She . . . she didn't want you to work?

Pause.

Tom And now them kids in 'infirmary. What have I

done? (*Pause.*) What can I do?

Scene Two

The kitchen and yard. About half an hour later. **Cath** *is stood at the kitchen door, looking out at the shed.* **Rainy** *is sat at the table.* **Chris** *is in the yard, sitting on the bench.* **Duane** *comes through the house into the kitchen, rattling a dice cup, followed by* **Linda**.

Duane   What we doing, then? Are we playing or what?

Rainy   You've won, haven't you?

Duane   Not yet. I thought you were just going to 'toilet?

Rainy   Nobody's got any money left.

Duane   Sell summat, then.

Rainy   I don't want to play any more.

Duane   Just 'cause I'm winning. Mam?

Cath   What?

Duane   You take over from Rainy.

Cath   No.

Duane   I thought we were all gunna play some games? (*Pause. To* **Linda**.) What you doing?

Linda   I think I've had enough.

Duane (*to himself*)   Sod you, then. (*He bangs down the dice cup on the table and goes off.*)

Rainy (*to* **Cath**)   In't he coming in?

Cath   I don't know what he's doing.

Chris *gets up, goes to the shed. Knocks.*

Chris   Dad?

Tom (*off*)   What?

Chris   Come on.

Pause. No response. **Chris** *sits again.*

Cath (*calling to* **Tom**)   Do you want a cup of tea? (*Pause. She goes to the shed.*)

Are you all right? (*Pause. To* **Chris**.) Why couldn't you tell him it was all right?

Chris   Lie, you mean? Like you?

Cath   Shut it. Look where your bloody probing and prodding's got now.

Chris   All you've given me for months, all you've said to me and Linda. Crap from beginning to end. Don't I count for owt?

Cath   Your dad had to do what he thought was right.

Chris   And you stood by him and drove me out.

Cath   I drove you out? I thought it were love everlasting what took you away? Don't you start blaming me now. You bloody well love to turn things inside out, don't you? Every bugger's in the wrong but you. You're a selfish little sod that's got no sympathy for your parents at all. Look what you've done to him now.

Chris   He's done it himself.

Cath *turns and goes in.* **Chris** *gets up and follows her.*

Chris   I . . . am I not supposed to be a bit pissed off after I find out you didn't want him to carry on working?

Cath   I've supported him. That's it. Maybe in the beginning . . . but he needed me to . . . He's done what he thought was right.

Chris   You. You I'm on about.

Cath   When has anybody ever been bothered what I think?

Chris   What? I'm bothered. I wunt be asking, would I?

Pause.

Cath He's been a good father to you.

Chris I know.

Cath You know nowt. The man's your father and you know nothing about him.

Chris I'm learning.

Cath You don't know what I've had to put up with.

Chris What's that mean? (*Pause.*) Eh? (*Pause.*) He's never here.

Cath Aye, and how do you think I cope wi' that, not knowing if he's going to come home? Not knowing if when he walks out 'gate it's last time?

Chris You what?

Rainy Leaving us, you mean?

Cath *shakes her head.*

Chris What, then?

Pause.

Cath I've tried to get him to see a doctor, but he won't.

Chris What for?

Rainy Mam. Don't be daft. It's nowt.

Chris What's nowt?

Cath How do you know it's nowt if he won't see a doctor about it?

Rainy He's been getting pains in his chest.

Cath Can't sleep with it.

Chris It's all this.

Cath What?

Chris Thinking about this.

Cath He's ill.

Chris Aye.

Cath What's that mean?

Chris Nowt.

Cath What you saying?

Rainy It's in his head?

Chris No. No –

Rainy What, then?

Chris Worry's made him think he's ill. That's all I'm –

Cath You talk stupid. I know whether he's ill or not.

Chris He's ill because summat's telling him he's wrong.

Rainy Guilty conscience?

Chris I never –

Cath That's it! I've bloody well had it with you!

Chris What?

Cath You've not got one good thought for that man, have you?

Chris I never said – I only said what I reckon –

Cath Shut up! Shut your foul mouth up!

Chris Mam, I never –

Cath (*moving away*) Get away from me.

Chris What?

Cath Don't talk to me!

Chris I'm only saying –

Cath Don't talk to me! (*She rushes out into the yard.*)

Rainy Bloody hell, Chris.

Chris What? (*Pause, then he kicks out at a chair, sending it scuttling across the kitchen.*) Fuck it! Fuck it!

Pause. **Duane** *comes through, takes the bucket from under the sink, fills it with water, takes it out to the yard, comes back in again, goes through, comes out again, carrying rod, reel, set-up, with float attached. He comes out into the yard, begins to practise casting the float into the bucket.*

Duane What's Dad doing?

Cath *goes to the shed, knocks on door.*

Cath Tom? Come on, love, come on.

Tom *comes out of the shed with a spade and a sheet of paper on which is drawn a garden plan.*

Duane What you doing?

Tom Where's Chris?

Duane In 'kitchen.

Tom (*shouting*) Chris!

Chris *comes out.*

Cath (*to* **Tom**) What are you doing?

Tom (*to* **Chris**) Here. Look. (*He shows him the plan*)

Chris What is it?

Tom My plan.

Chris What for?

Tom For here. Out here.

Chris *examines the plan as* **Tom** *shows where he is planning to put things.* **Rainy** *and* **Linda** *stand at the kitchen door, watching.*

Pond's going to be here . . .

Duane We having a pond?

Tom Yes. (*To* **Chris**.) Your money. I'm buying one of them glass fibre ponds.

Duane We having fish in it?

Tom Yes. Get some fish. Little carp.

Duane Carp?

Tom Yes.

Duane Ace.

Tom All 'soil I take out, I'm building up round 'ere, like crescent shaped, make a rockery, get some nice rocks, put some stuff in it. I want it to look natural, though. Get some lilies in 'pond, irises growing on 'edge. Little patio. Crazy paving.

Duane Can we have a barbecue?

Tom Yes. I could put that down yonder.

Duane Ace. Barbecued carp.

Tom And I want some trees. (*Referring to the plan.*) These here, these are shrubs. These here, they're trees. Natural trees. I want it natural. Might get some ash trees, eh? What do you think? (*Pause.*) Gunna cost a fair bit, when it's all done, but it'll look nice, won't it?

Duane It'll look ace, won't it Rainy?

Tom (*to* **Rainy**) Won't want to go on holiday when I've done. You can sit out here. I don't want no patio furniture, though. I don't want plastic. Wood. Rustic, like.

Duane I can get some wood.

Tom Can you?

Cath No he can't.

Duane I can. (*To* **Tom**.) It waint cost owt.

Tom I don't mind spending. Get some real good stuff. Proper preserved.

Duane You could make a trellis.

Tom No. No, it's got to be natural looking. I want to attract wildlife, see. Birds and that. Like a little nature reserve. It'd be champion. (*To* **Cath**.) What d' you reckon?

Cath Well it'd keep you busy.

Duane It'd get smashed up.

Tom Well we'll put a fence up, then, won't we? Ten foot fucking high, if need be! Shift, I want to mark out where 'pond's going.

Duane *moves the bucket away.*

Chris Why ash trees, Dad?

Tom *begins to mark the soil with the spade.*

Cath You can't start now.

Tom Yes I can. Give me some idea what's what. I've thought about 'little un an' all, Linda, wi' pond. I'll like make a little wall round so she can't fall in. I'd be out 'ere anyroad, watching. I'll keep an eye on her, make sure she doesn't fall in or owt, hurt herself on 'stones. It'd be her little wild garden, eh? Place to come and watch nature.

Chris Dad . . .

Tom I want to do it. I want to, all right?

Pause.

Chris Do you want me to help?

Tom No. No, thanks, Chris.

Chris I'd like to.

Tom I want to do it missen. All on it missen, like. (*He continues to mark out the pond.*)

Chris It's a good idea, Dad. (*To* **Duane**.) In't it?

Duane Yea. Ace.

Chris (*to* **Cath**) In't it?

Cath How the hell you going to manage lifting stones about?

Tom I'm not a bloody weakling.

Pause.

Chris   It'll look great.

Cath   It'll be a change, I suppose.

Pause.

Duane   Fishing in me own back yard.

Cath *goes in the kitchen, sits at the table.* **Rainy** *moves across to her. Long pause.*

Rainy   Shall I make some tea?

Cath *shakes her head. Pause.*

Does he want my holiday money back?

Cath   He's not getting it. That's yours. That's yours.

Rainy   I just thought.

Cath   What does he think he's doing? Barmy apeth.

Rainy   It'll keep him busy.

Cath   Aye.

Rainy   Keep him occupied.

Pause.

Linda   This is for her, isn't it?

Rainy   Yes.

Pause.

Cath   He's not a bad man.

Rainy   Nobody said he was.

Cath (*to* **Linda**)   Just a bit . . . like a lot of folk. Lost.

Pause. She picks up the dice cup, shakes the dice in it, tips them out. She does this twice more.

Rainy   Shall we have a game?

Cath   No.

Rainy   Come on. Summat to do.

Cath Keep us occupied?

Rainy (*to* **Linda**) Only way we'll have any property.

Cath Aye. (*Pause.*) Bloody council house and he's planning to spend all that.

Rainy Let him.

Cath Aye. Only money, eh?

Rainy Can't take it with you.

Cath Where are we going?

Pause.

Rainy Come on, let's play.

Cath I'm having the top hat.

Rainy *goes through inner door.* **Linda** *goes to the yard door.*

Linda Duane?

Duane What?

Linda Monopoly. You playing?

Duane Yea.

Linda Come on, then.

She moves back in. **Rainy** *comes through with the Monopoly board. They begin to set it up.*

Duane Dad?

Tom What?

Duane You know your rod and reel?

Tom What about 'em?

Chris He wants to do a swap.

Duane Eh?

Chris Swap you his gear for yours. He wants to have your old gear, since he's only an amateur, you have his.

Duane   No I don't.

Tom   You keep what you've got. What's up wi' it? Aren't you satisfied?

Duane   Yea.

Tom   Well, then.

Duane   It were him said it, not me.

Tom   Anyroad, I wouldn't let anybody fish wi' that rod o' mine. I've had that rod since I were eighteen. My dad bought me that rod.

Chris   Did he?

Tom   He did.

Pause. They watch **Tom**. *He is busy with his planning.*

Duane   I'm off in. (*He picks up the bucket, rod, makes to go in.*)

Chris (*to* **Duane**)   Grapple hook and rope.

Duane   You what?

Chris   Tomorrow. We'll drag it out.

Duane   Oh. Right. Do you reckon?

Chris   Yes.

Duane   We could do wi' that woman in that advert, cunt we? You know, her what comes up out the water wi' that sword. Where all them women are doing upside down dancing.

Chris   Yea.

Duane   I should 'ave 'ad a can. I'd a smacked 'em all in. Picked 'em all up together and chucked 'em in 'water. Bubbles coming up. 'I bet he drinks Carling Black Label.'

He goes in, empties the bucket as the women set out the Monopoly game. **Chris** *watches* **Tom**.

Tom   How's it looking?

Chris You can see what it's going to look like.

Tom Can you?

Chris You can.

Tom You can can't you?

Chris Yea. (*Pause.*) Do you want a mug of tea?

Tom Aye. Yes, I will.

Chris *goes into the kitchen. Fills kettle, puts it on.*

Rainy Yes, please.

Cath Yes, please.

Linda Yes, please, Chris.

Duane We got any beer?

Cath No.

Duane (*to* **Chris**) Yes, please.

Chris *puts the tea in the pot. In the yard,* **Tom** *begins to whistle to himself. It is Marvin Gaye's* Abraham, Martin and John.

All of You Mine

All of You Mine was first performed at the Bush Theatre on 8 January 1997, with the following cast:

Verna	Marion Bailey
Cissy	Anne Carroll
Earl	Andrew Dunn
Danum	David Hounslow
Alma	Melanie Kilburn
Billy	Roy North
Neville	Lee Oakes

Directed by Simon Usher
Designed by Anthony Lamble
Lighting by Paul Russell
Sound by Paul Bull

Characters

Cissy Cade, *fifty-nine, well worn, widow*

Danum Cade, *thirty-nine, Cissy's son, ex-miner, now owns and runs a garden centre*

Verna Cade, *thirty-seven, Cissy's eldest daughter, single, with one son, twelve*

Alma Bentley, *thirty-five, Cissy's youngest daughter, works for Danum, married to*

Earl Bentley, *thirty-eight, ex-miner, self taught mechanic*

Neville Bentley, *sixteen, son of Alma and Earl*

Billy Winder, *fifty-five, ex-miner, now a car park attendant at the garden centre*

Time The present. Summer, and events during the miners' strike of 1984.

Setting

Any one of fourteen ex-pit villages around Doncaster, South Yorkshire, whose pits were closed either as a planned programme, or as a direct result of the 1984 miners' strike. Some have seen the emergence of 'business parks', where businesses receive cheap rentals for one or two years, and pay rock bottom casual labour wages, with no security, before they move on. Others have seen more enterprising efforts by the redundant miners themselves – one ex-pit is actually now a thriving garden centre owned by six ex-miners who pooled their redundancy. One slag heap is now, in fact, to be the site of the Earth Centre – a vast complex and nature reserve dedicated to environmental issues.

Cissy's back yard. A terraced house, with a ramshackle porch/veranda on which are pot plants, hanging baskets. A step down into a derelict, dry yard.

Act One – Friday

Summer. Now. **Cissy***'s back yard. At the back of the terraced house there is a ramshackle porch/veranda affair, with a step down to the yard itself, which is barren and dry. Two hanging baskets on brackets are fastened to the porch, a few pot plants nearby.*

Scene One

Mid-day

Cissy *is sat out in an old armchair soaking up the sun, dozing. She wears glasses. She has a bandage round one leg.* **Alma** *arrives. She wears a nylon smock/dress, the type worn by supermarket ladies with her name tag pinned over her breast. She carries a plastic bag. When she reaches* **Cissy** *she takes out a white geranium in a pot, teases out the leaves a little, then places it among the others.*

Cissy (*opening her eyes*)   It smells pink. Is it pink?

Alma   White.

Cissy   You're late, aren't you?

Alma   We've been busy.

Cissy   Everything's frazzling. I can hear 'em groaning for a drink.

Alma   I'll do it tonight when it's cooler. It'll kill them now.

Cissy   I'm wilting myself.

Alma *goes inside.*

Kids have been out of school long since. They've got fish. I smelt it cooking. (*Pause.*) I don't want any dinner. (*Pause.*) I'll have some of that jungle juice.
I think Long Shanks and her 'usband must have taken 'kids to Bridlington again. She normally speaks when she's taking 'em to school. She said the other week they might try and get same caravan they got last year. It'll be nice for 'em,

won't it? If it's like this. Picked it right. I don't know what he does. They seem to 'ave money for 'olidays, though. If it's like this it'll be nice.

Alma *comes out with a drink in a glass.*

Have you decided yet?

Alma   No.

Cissy   I'm going to need to know.

Alma   It won't be yet awhile. After September, when it slackens off. Might get away then.

Cissy   You want to. Do you good, all of you. Won't be many more years before Neville won't want to be going on holiday with his mam and dad.

Alma   He doesn't want to now.

Cissy   Well maybe that's what you want, on your own the pair of you. Get yourselves abroad somewhere.

Alma   Earl's not keen.

Cissy   Neville could stop wi' me.

Alma   We'll see.

Cissy   I would if I could.

Alma   You?

Cissy   I would.

Alma   I thought you were terrified of flying?

Cissy   Your father's not here now, is he? If I'm going to go I'm going to go. (*Pause.*) Not that I've anybody to go with, so that's that. No, you get yourself off. You'll enjoy it. I can manage with just the home help for a fortnight I'm sure. Only I'm going to need to tell her.

Alma *puts the drink in* **Cissy***'s hand.*

This bandage is strangling me. She's a nice enough lass but she's not got much idea. Me foot's gone dead. I said to

her, leave it off, let a bit of sun get to it. I can't
understand why the bugger's taking so long to heal up.
Least bloody knock and you're laid up like this. Will you
loosen it for me?

Alma   It's meant to be tight.

Pause. **Cissy** *drinks.*

Cissy   I've gone off tea.

Alma   Oh?

Cissy   I'm sure she puts three in that pot in a morning.
Only needs two. I don't like to say owt. It's too strong for
me.

Alma   She won't know if you don't tell her.

Cissy   I don't like. She's a good lass. She's a Godsend to
me.

Alma   I'll get a bigger box, then, when I go.

Cissy   Would you?

Alma   Yes.

Cissy   And a packet of nice biscuits.

Alma   You don't eat biscuits.

Cissy   She might fancy one. Least I can do, all she does
for me.

Alma   It's her job, she's paid for it.

Cissy   Aye, and I'm grateful for it. (*Pause.*) She's divorced.
She's on her own in one of them flats on Littlemoor Lane.
Her mother used to look after that launderette, top of
Burton Avenue. Thin woman, always had a fag on. Dangly
ears. Do you remember her?

Alma   No.

Cissy   You do. Ginger. Always had a tight perm. Looked
like a woolly hat.

Alma   I can't remember.

Cissy   You've a shocking memory. It used to be a cobbler's.

Alma   What did?

Cissy   That launderette. Years ago. I used to like to go in just to hear the bell on the back of the door. Little old bloke. Dead now. Mr Trueman. Hunchback. Tapping his little hammer. Used to smell lovely. I've only to smell shoe leather now and I can see him. (*Pause.*) All them little shops along there are gone now. Do you remember Rose's cake shop?

Alma   Yes.

Cissy   She did all your birthdays. That day I came home and you were playing under 'kitchen table and I didn't see you and I said to your dad, 'Oh, no, I've forgot the effin' cake.'

Alma   Mam.

Cissy   What?

Alma   You've got it wrong. It wasn't me. It was Verna.

Cissy   It was you. I remember who it was.

Alma   It was Verna.

Cissy   I'm telling you. You can't remember that?

Alma   Yes.

Cissy   If your dad were here he'd tell you.

Pause.

Alma   I don't think I can bike back up that hill in this. (*Heat.*)

Cissy   You ought to get your test passed. I wish I'd done it. Too late now. Would have been nice to get out. I go nowhere now. I see nobody. Only place I drive myself is up the wall. If your dad were here to see me like this he'd have a fit. He would. Wouldn't he? We went all over together.

Alma   Eh?

Cissy   You know we did, what's the matter with you?

Alma   First I knew.

Cissy   That little three-wheeler we 'ad.

Alma   I were still at school then.

Cissy   Jumbles. Car boots. Your dad used to hate it. I miss me bargains. You've had many a bit of good gear off me one time or another, you know you have.

Alma   Earl says Danum's thinking about doing car boots up at the garden centre. Back end.

Cissy   Oh aye? Well that's not so far away for me, is it?

Alma   No.

Cissy   If you got Earl to take me up in the van.

Alma   What about all the pushing and shoving? You don't want to be laid up again.

Cissy   I'm deadly wi' these elbows when I spot a bargain.

Alma   How are you going to see stuff?

Cissy   You're a real comfort to me, do you know that?

Alma   I'm sorry.

Cissy   I should hope I'm not going to be stuck here for ever, like this.

Alma   'Course you won't.

Cissy   If I thought that.

Pause.

Alma   I'll come round tonight. Water everything.

Cissy   If it's not given up before then. (*Pause.*) If it's like this on Sunday it'll be nice.

Alma Won't it.

Cissy Be a few there.

Alma I expect so.

Cissy Brass band.

Alma They've started setting it all out.

Cissy Have they?

Alma I'll take you if you're up to it.

Cissy No, no. I can't stand for long. You go.

Alma There'll be seats to sit down.

Cissy What, them fold up things? If I sit on one o' them I'll never get up again. Anyway, if it's like this I shall be stuck to the bugger permanent.

Alma You sure you don't mind me going?

Cissy 'Course I don't mind. Why should I? More folk go the better. You'll have to take some photographs.

Alma I don't know if you're allowed.

Cissy 'Course you're allowed.

Alma Well it's a service, like, as well, in't it? Vicar and that.

Cissy You've got to 'ave a mimento.

Alma Yes.

Cissy It won't all be a sad and solemn do. They wouldn't want that, would they?

Alma No. (**Alma** *takes her glass, moves to go in.*)

Cissy What's Earl doing?

Alma I don't know. I 'aven't asked 'im. (**Alma** *goes in.*)

Cissy *closes her eyes.*

Cissy Billy Winder's let his pigeons out.

Mr Magpie was here this morning. Well there were a few of 'em, row they were making. I don't know what it was about but summat was aggravating 'em. Could have been a cat. What is it? One for sorrow, two for joy, three for a girl, four for a boy.
Three or four of 'em. Must have been.

Alma *comes out.*

Can you see 'pigeons?

Alma   No.

Cissy   They're up there. Coming round in a minute.

Alma   I'll see you, Mam. (*She walks away. Stops. Looks up.*) They're here now.

Looks at **Cissy**. *Her eyes are closed. She is smiling.* **Alma** *goes.* **Cissy** *sleeps.*

Cissy   We 'ad some smashing 'olidays at Bridlington, didn't we?

The scene fades.

Scene Two

The same. Mid afternoon.

Cissy   Pull the chain after you!
My first job were a wages clerk at Woodyard. Every Thursday afternoon there'd be a queue a mile long of fellas whose wages I'd worked out wrong. It were all pounds, shillings and pence then. You had a ready reckoner. Six and ninepence three-farthings an hour or whatever, depending on the job, and then so much for overtime. I never did get it right. I learnt a few swear words off my boss, I can tell you. Little Polish bloke. Hugo Spielvogel. He were lovely. He'd rant and rave at me one minute then bring me in a Kit-kat. Had an 'eart attack one afternoon. Thursday probably. I ran down the yard to fetch the first aider. I couldn't find him anywhere. I found him in 'finish

with some lass behind a stack of sash windows. Hugo were
blue when we got back.

Neville *comes out of the house.*

You want to watch out for yourself up at 'garden centre.
They can be buggers wi' new lads startin'.

Neville 'Ow come?

Cissy Teasin' and what 'ave you. They can be a rum
lot. Your mam'll tell you. (*Pause.*) What you bin doing?

Neville Eh? When?

Cissy You've bin long enough going to the toilet.

Neville Oh. Sorry.

Cissy You bin down my purse again?

Neville No.

Cissy If you want money, ask. I've told you before.

Neville I don't want any money.

Cissy Fetch me my purse.

Neville I don't want any money.

Cissy It's in 'middle drawer.

Neville *goes in.*

I don't like to see you going without. I know what you
young lads get up to. Lassing it and what have you. You
got yourself one yet? (*Pause.*) I'm beginning to think there's
summat the matter wi' you. And don't go spending it on
fags, neither. You know what I think about that. Think of
your grandad.
Mind you, they said that's what it was, but it were coal
dust, biggest part. They had to say that otherwise they
might have had to pay out. Rasping and wheezing. Nights
I've given 'im a dig in bed. Sounded like some bugger
playing bagpipes underwater. Aye. Now I'd give everything
I had for the sound of him beside me.

Neville *comes out with the purse, gives it to* **Cissy**.

Do you miss your grandad?

Neville Sometimes.

Cissy He'd be pleased to think you still came round to see me, wouldn't he?

Neville I dunno.

Cissy Here. (*Opens purse.*) Have a look for me. (*Offers him the purse.*) What is there?

Neville I don't want it.

Cissy (*taking out a note*) What's this?

Neville A fiver.

Cissy Here, tek it. (*She grabs his arm, shoves the fiver in his hand.*)

Neville Thanks. (*He pockets it.*)

Billy Winder *comes up the path, carrying a plastic bag, whistling.*

Cissy Now then, Billy.

Billy Cissy. All right, Neville?

Neville All right.

Billy (*to* **Cissy**) I've brought thee a lettuce and some rhubarb. Where's tha want it?

Cissy Oh, thanks, Billy. Just leave it here. Thank you.

Billy Thought your Alma could set to and make you a pie. (*To* **Neville**.) Now then.

Neville All right?

Billy (*to* **Cissy**) A free man now, then?

Cissy Eh?

Billy Finished school.

Cissy Aye. Best years of your life if you did but know it.

Neville   Oh. That's it, then. If 'rest's no better than what's bin . . .

Cissy   You'll know what I'm on about one day.

Billy   It's just beginning for 'im.

Cissy   Aye. Starts Monday.

Billy   Lookin' forward to it?

Neville   Dunno. It's all plants, innit?

Billy   Your mam'll be pleased.

Neville   She is. They'll 'ave to find summat else to row about then.

Billy   Your mam's got a lot on.

Neville   Yea.

Cissy   She's never 'ere more than five minutes.

Billy   Now come on, Ciss.

Cissy   Aye, go on, say it.

Billy   What?

Cissy   Well I won't be here much longer to be looked after.

Billy   You'll outlive all of us.

Cissy   I bloody well hope not.

Neville   I'm off. See you.

Cissy   Behave yourself.

Billy   See you, Neville.

Neville *goes.*

Cissy   He wants putting in a sack and shaking up, that lad.

Billy   Give over.

Cissy   No go in 'im. Mopes about . . .

Billy He's all right.

Cissy He's not interested in anything.

Billy 'Course he is. He dunt know it yet, that's all.

Cissy That's a queer way of puttin' it. You talk to 'im about it and it's as if you're spoon feeding 'im wi' dog shit.

Billy You wait and see. He's a good lad.

Cissy He ought to be bloody grateful 'e's got summat. Most on 'em 'is age, there's bugger all for 'em. No wonder they 'ang about street corners. I feel sorry for 'em.

Billy Aye. Them wi' any sense move away. (*Pause.*) How are you, then?

Cissy I'm still here.

Billy You getting on wi' them specs any better?

Cissy Na. They don't make a scrap o' difference. Like I'm looking through a waterfall at a black and white telly.

Billy You're not having 'em seen to, then?

Cissy They're not laying me out on no operating table for a forty percent chance of it doing any good. I'm past being poked and prodded about.

Billy Aye. Still, tha dunt miss much of what's going on, Cissy.

Cissy Nowt else to do, sitting here hour after hour. My arse is red raw. (*Pause.*) How's 'allotment doing, then?

Billy Could do wi' a good downpour.

Cissy Aye. Freshen everything up a bit. I heard your pigeons having a fly round.

Billy Eh?

Cissy Dinner time.

Billy I've not 'ad pigeons for years, Cissy.

Cissy Somebody's got some.

Billy Not me. I never got no more after 'last lot went. Somebody's pigeon pie.

Cissy Aye, well, it were probably 'first bit o' meat they had for weeks.

Billy I suppose so. (*Pause.*) Seems another world, Cissy.

Cissy Some folk have short memories.

Billy Aye, well.

Cissy That's my downfall. I've too good a memory.

Pause.

Billy There were some good times in there an' all, want there?

Verna *appears.*

You had two smashing lasses, Cissy. Both on 'em. Still 'ave.

Cissy Eh?

Billy Alma and Verna.

Cissy Who's talking about her?

Billy I'm just saying.

Cissy What's she come into your 'ead for? Give me some grief over 'years I know that.

Billy Remember that time she split 'er 'ead open? Fell off them sewage pipes they were layin' in Arthur Street? An' I carried 'er 'ome, laid her out on your back kitchen table?

Cissy Aye, it's seen a few things 'as that table.

Billy I come across 'er in 'street one day, cryin' 'er eyes out, searchin' up and down kerb edge. 'Now then, what's up?' I said. 'I've lost me scab,' she said, 'I can't find me scab.' She thought if she fun it an' put it back on her knee, it wouldn't scar.

Cissy What's brought her up all of a sudden?

Billy I don't know. I were just thinkin'. That's all, you know. The boy she had by Joe, whether he's like her, into everything. (*Pause.*) I'm sorry, Ciss, I shunt 'ave. Forget I said owt.

Cissy I 'ave.

Pause.

Billy I were just thinking, that's all. Sunday.

Cissy She'll not show 'er face. No fear o' that.

Billy No. (*Pause.*) Must be 'ottest we've 'ad. Not far off.

Cissy You ought to 'ave an 'at on. Sun's got to you.

Billy Aye. (*Pause.*) I'm watering twice a day up yon.

Cissy Worth it. Can't beat a bit of 'ome grown.

Billy No. Well let me know if you want any. I'll 'ave 'runners ready soon.

Cissy Aye, I will. Good of you. Do you want an 'at?

Billy Eh?

Cissy It's a summer 'at. One of Frank's. I kept it.

Billy No, no, I'm not one for 'ats.

Cissy It's a good un. Proper straw. Too good to chuck out. 'Ave it.

Billy No.

Cissy *gets up.*

No, Cissy. You don't 'ave to gi' me owt.

Cissy I'm going to 'toilet. You sure?

Billy You've given me enough o' Frank's gear one time or another.

Cissy Suit yourself.

Billy I'll get off, then. (*He makes a move.*)

Cissy Aye, all right. I shall enjoy me rhubarb pie.

Billy Anytime. Do you want 'and?

Cissy I can manage.

She goes in. **Billy** *stands a moment, looking round, then goes off down the yard. The scene fades to the sound of two young girls singing* The Clapping Song *and laughing.*

Scene Three

The same. Early evening.

Earl *comes out of the house with a watering can full of water. He puts it down, sits in* **Cissy**'s *chair, relaxes for a moment before* **Alma** *comes out.* **Alma** *picks up the can.*

Alma She's lying down. When are you going to put her bed downstairs?

Earl When she gets out of it.

Alma Tonight?

Earl Your Danum'll give us 'and with it.

Alma (*watering the plants*) What did he say, then? Was he pleased?

Earl Pleased?

Alma Wasn't he? Why? Hearing his sister's turned up?

Earl He just said 'oh'.

Alma 'Oh'?

Earl What's he supposed to say?

Alma Well he must have said something.

Earl He said she must be here for the do.

Alma Well of course she's here for the do.

Earl I'm just saying what he said.

Alma Look, when she does decide to come round, just –

Earl You think she will?

Alma I just want things to be all right.

Earl She won't. What, 'ere d'you mean or our 'ouse?

Alma Either. (*Pause.*) To think I were only thinking about her this dinner. Then somebody tells me they've seen her.

Earl Aye.

Alma That's real strange, that is.

Earl What?

Alma I said it's real strange.

Earl What is?

Alma I wonder if the boy's like her or Joe?

Earl If it is his.

Alma 'Course it's his.

Earl Your mother won't see her. You know that, don't you?

Pause.

Alma Maybe I should go round.

Earl What?

Alma Joe's mother's. Where she's staying. Maybe I should go round.

Earl No.

Alma Why not?

Earl I'm not 'avin you 'ot footin' it round their 'ouse as if everything's all right.

Alma Why shouldn't it be?

Earl Think about your mother.

Alma When have you ever been bothered about her?

Earl She waint want you suddenly starting things up as if twelve years were nowt.

Alma What would you care? If me mother never spoke to us again, it'd be too soon for you.

Earl I wouldn't care. You would.

Alma Since when have you – ?

Earl I'm just tellin' you! Wait on and see. (*Pause.*) She might have no intention of seein' any of her own family. You go round there all set to start up where you left off and she might slam 'door in your face. Think on. Wait for 'er to make a move.

Alma I shall 'ave to see her Sunday, won't I? (*She looks at him.*)

Earl Aye. You step in first and you might get a gob full for your trouble.

Alma *waters the plants.*

Every Christmas you wait for a card you never get, finish up in a state over it, then decide she's not worth it, till next year. When are you going to realize? She dunt want owt to do wi' any of us. We're all right as we are, wi' out 'er.

Danum *arrives.*

All right?

Danum Yea. Alma.

She doesn't respond. **Danum** *moves up the yard, stands against the porch.*

Alma She's asleep.

Danum You seen her?

Alma Who?

Danum Who do you think?

Alma   No. Have you?

Danum   No. (*Pause.* **Danum** *looks at the plants.*)

Alma   They're all paid for. Do you want to see the receipts?

Danum   What's up wi' you?

Earl   How's 'car?

Danum   I walked.

Earl   I told you. Bring it round. I'll have a look at it.

Danum   I'm not lettin' you put yer 'ands on it.

Earl   Suit yourself.

Danum   Do you know how much that car cost me?

Alma   We don't want to know. Do you think we're interested?

Danum (*to* **Earl**)   Too much for you to prat about on it.

Earl   They're all 'same under 'bonnet.

Danum   It's not a bloody pick-up truck.

Earl   It got me 'ere though, didn't it?

Cissy (*off*)   Hello? Hello! Who is it? What's goin' off?

Alma   It's only us, Mam. (*She goes in.*)

Danum   She's not been in touch, then?

Earl   Eh?

Danum   Alma. Not gone round.

Earl   No. She just told you. I telled her to keep away, like you said.

Danum   Will she?

Earl   I can't do no more than tell her. (*Pause.*) Somebody in 'paper shop tonight telled me they'd seen her.

Danum   Getting out and about, then.

Earl Looks like. (*Pause.*) Said they'd seen her up at 'cemetery this morning.

Danum Seeing Joe?

Earl Must a bin.

Danum Wouldn't be to see me dad, would it?

Earl 'Ad some'dy with 'er an all.

Danum The boy?

Earl Him, yes. They were with Billy Winder. (*Pause.*) What's she seeing him for?

Danum How the bloody hell should I know? (*Pause.*) I'll collar 'im tomorrow.

Earl *looks at him.*

He works for me.

Earl Billy?

Danum Week-ends. Car park attendant. Cash in 'and.

Earl I didn't know. He come asking for work?

Danum No. I went to 'im.

Earl Why?

Danum We're busy.

Earl I wouldn't a thought –

Danum I sent somebody round to ask 'im.

Earl Oh.

Danum Now he's working for me.

Earl Yea.

Danum Can't I do somebody a favour?

Earl Yea. Good idea.

Danum What?

Earl   No, it's a . . . best thing. (*Pause.*) I can't fathom it.

Danum   She's here for Sunday.

Earl   That's all? It's Friday, though, innit?

The light changes. The yard, twelve years ago. Afternoon. **Verna** *appears from the house.* **Verna** *is six months pregnant.*

Verna (*calling back*)   See you, then, Mam. Bye. (*She comes down into the yard.*) See you, Danum.

Danum   Yea. Take care.

Verna (*tapping her stomach*)   I will.

Danum   I mean it. All of you.

She stops.

Verna   What's up? Danum? What's the matter?

Danum   Will you have a word with Joe?

Verna   About? (*Pause.*) You know? How?

Danum   Never mind how.

Verna   And? Danum, what's wrong?

Danum   Listen, we never had this conversation. All right? You got nowt from me.

Verna   I 'aven't yet.

Danum   I'm just telling you, Verna. You have to get him to come off that list.

Verna   Why?

Danum   Because if he doesn't, they'll get to him, make sure he doesn't go down.

Verna   What? He's volunteered for a safety check! What are you saying?

Danum   The Board's payin' forty-seven volunteers way over the odds, for the job.

Verna   Every one of 'em would do it for nothing. You

know that.

Danum I know that. Board know that. That's why they're paying 'em. It's a deliberate tactic to rile us. What's other forty-seven thousand next to bloody starvation supposed to think, eh?

Verna You're saying they know the union will stop it 'appening? (*Pause.*) Why do that? To shut the pit altogether? Delay the safety check till it's too late to save it? Is that what you're saying they want? Danum? If you know that's what they're up to then all the more reason to make sure it's done. Let 'em go down. If I can work that out, why can't your lot? Danum?

Danum They can't see it. They don't want to see it. You think they want to start believing that pit's never goin' to open again after they've fought for all this time? All they can see is a smack in the face when 'news breaks how much they're payin' forty-seven blokes for a day's work. It's an insult to 'em. They're gonna do everything they can to stop it, with or without union be'ind 'em.

Verna You know every man on that list. Don't you? Don't you? How? It was all supposed to be done in secret. Nobody knew who they were. Where did you get the names from?

Danum I thought I was 'elpin' you telling you this, that's all.

Verna Who do you know?

Danum Do you want to see him in 'ospital?

Verna You're just animals. That's all you are. Animals. You make me sick to look at you.

Danum What am I supposed to do, just let it 'appen? You're my sister. All I'm tellin' you is you've −

Verna I'll tell you what you're telling me. A man what's bin loyal to this strike from the start, stood on 'same picket line wi' you, travelled the country wi' you, pulled 'police off

you when you were gettin' your 'ead kicked in, you're after
sorting him out as if he's just another common scab!

Danum   Just tell Joe if he even starts walking in the
direction of that pit, they'll nail his fucking feet to the floor.
All right? Plain enough? So get him off the list or get him
out, sod off somewhere. Think what you want, I can't help
that, only think on – I didn't want any of this to 'appen. I
swear. If I'd a known Joe had put his name down ... if
they find out I've talked to you ...

She moves off.

Verna! Verna! What you doin', then? Verna!

The light changes back.

Earl   What's she up to?

Cissy (*off*)   I don't want 'er round 'ere.

Alma (*off*)   No.

Cissy *comes out, walking with a stick.* **Alma** *follows.*

Cissy   I don't want her 'ere. Do you hear me?

Earl (*to* **Alma**)   I told you.

Cissy   You keep your nose out. (*To* **Danum**.) I knew you
were 'ere. 'Smell woke me up.

Danum   Eh?

Cissy   You've got that puff gear on again. It knocks your
'ead off that aftershave you wear.

Earl *laughs.*

(*To* **Earl**.) I don't know which is worse, that or axle grease.

Alma   She's brought her boy, Mam.

Cissy   Oh and that's going to change everything, is it?
How can he be a grandson to me when I've never seen
him? She forgot us faster than we forgot her. Just
remember that.

Alma   I do.

Cissy   That's all you need keep in yer 'ead. And if you've any thought for me, you won't go near neither. None of you.

Danum   I don't want to see her. We thought we'd best tell you before you found out from other folk.

Cissy   It's a wonder some bugger ant bin round to tell me all about it already. Break their bloody necks to be 'first round 'ere. What's folk supposed to think, her parading him about streets and them knowing full well she's not bin to see her own mother? Because they will know. Mek it their business to. What are they going to be thinking?

Danum   Who cares what they think?

Cissy   I see 'em every day. You're up yonder, aren't you? Nobody ever has 'time o' day for you up there anyway. Just sit and twitch behind 'net curtains. You say 'hello' and it's as if you've just farted. Everybody's in one another's pockets round 'ere. Or have you forgotten already?

Danum   Let 'em think what they want, long as you know what's what.

Cissy   You don't have to rely on 'em day in day out. I'm in no fit state to do for myself. I wish I was.

Danum   So what are you saying, then?

Cissy   Eh?

Danum   What are you saying?

Cissy   I'm not saying anything. I'm just saying. (*Pause. She sits.*) All this time. All these years. I swore to your dad I'd never ever forgive 'er for not coming to his funeral. And I won't. That's what finally put 'tin lid on it. I don't want to see 'er. I've let go now of whatever it was I had left to hold onto. And now I've done it, it's done. You think what you want, lass. I know what you think. It's not come from wanting it, it's a case of having to, to keep from going round the bend.

Alma I know that.

Cissy I don't care who tells 'er, long as she knows what's what. Comin' back 'ere. I don't want 'er 'ere. Can't come to her own dad's do, but she can turn up out of the blue for Joe. What's she wantin'? Everybody's attention on 'er? Feelin' sorry for 'er, weepin' and wailin'?

Pause.

Danum So how do we keep her away from you?

Alma She won't come 'ere. She knows what she'll get.

Danum What, you think we should throw a party?

Alma I'll see her, warn her off.

Cissy Not likely.

Alma Why not?

Cissy I'll not 'ave you eyeing me every day as if you 'ate me for it.

Earl Why don't you just write her a note? I'll tek it. Shove it through 'letter box.

Alma You won't go nowhere. You're not a bloody messenger boy.

Cissy I wouldn't waste good notepaper.

Danum It's got to come from you, Mam, one way or 'other. We can't mek 'er go when it's you she's come to see.

Cissy What would I put? I can't see to put owt.

Danum I'll write it.

Alma (*to* **Earl**) You're not tekin a note!

Cissy (*to* **Danum**) Would you?

Danum You tell me what you want.

Cissy (*to* **Alma**)   There's a Basildon Bond in 'middle drawer.

Alma *doesn't move.*

Alma.

Verna *arrives.*

Cissy   What's up? Who's here?

Alma   Hello, Verna.

Verna   Hello, Alma. (*Pause.*) Hello, Mam. (*Pause.*) Your flowers look nice. Danum. You look well. Earl. Put on a bit of weight. (*Pause.*) All here. I got here last night.

Cissy   You're a few years too late, lass.

Verna *is crying a little now.* **Alma** *moves to her.* **Verna** *wants to hold her. She is not sure what to do.* **Alma** *hugs her.*

Cissy   Am I going to get this bed shifted, then?

Alma *and* **Verna** *move apart a little.*

Earl   What, now?

Cissy   Yes. Alma.

Alma   Danum can do it.

Cissy   You can fetch 'sheets down. (*Pause.*) Alma.

Alma   No.

Cissy   I want the three of you. Inside or outside altogether.

Earl *and* **Danum** *go in.* **Alma** *follows. Pause.*

Verna   I was ill, Mam. I went into hospital just before dad died. I never got the letter from Joe's mam till it was too late. I didn't know. I would have come. I would.

Cissy   He was dying for two years. (*Pause.*) 'She'll come,' he'd say. 'Don't be like that. She'll come.'

Verna   Why didn't you write to me?

Cissy   P'raps because I didn't know where you were.

Verna   Joe's parents knew. You could have –

Pause.

Cissy   They knew. Your own mother ...

Verna   Please, Mam, all I want is to –

Cissy   Oh, you're after summat, then?

Verna   I want to tell you why. (*Pause.*) I've wanted to tell you why all ... through all this. I can't – (*Through a choked sob.*) It's too late to tell.

Cissy   What? I didn't hear you?

Verna *is crying.*

Verna   It's too late to tell.

Cissy   So what do you want, then? (*A long pause.* **Cissy** *can't let it go.*) What do you call him, then?

Verna   Joe. Joe Junior. JJ. Everybody calls him JJ.

Cissy   Who's he tek after?

Verna   His dad.

Cissy   Does he?

Verna   Sometimes I can see my dad in him.

Cissy   Aye?

Verna   Sometimes.

Cissy *takes off her glasses, takes a tissue from up her sleeve, wipes her eyes then her glasses. She tries but fails to make it look routine.*

Cissy   I wish you'd have brought him to see him. (*Pause.*) I can't forgive you for that, lass.

Verna   I couldn't.

Cissy   Couldn't? Why not? What stopped you? What did I do? (*Pause.*) What have I or your father ever done wrong to you?

Verna You did nothing.

Cissy Well, then. (*Pause.*) What are you saying?

Verna What?

Cissy What the bloody hell could we do? Is that it? Is that why?

Verna No.

Cissy If that's what this has all bin about –

Verna Please, Mam. Please. Leave it alone. I haven't said it were 'cos of you.

Cissy Who then? Danum?

Verna Mam, I've left all this behind, long since. I've bin – the longer it got, the more I wanted back, but couldn't, didn't dare, because I knew I'd get all this.

Cissy And you think you don't deserve this?

Verna Yes. I do.

Cissy What do you think I've bin like over it? Eh? You will never know. Never. You haven't the slightest notion. Dug an 'ole in me as big as Cantley Quarry. Emptied me out. Finished your father off. And you're hoping there's summat left for you when you come waltzing back? Forget what's gone on, pick up where we left off as if you've just bin down 'shop for a bread loaf?

Verna *is crying. A long pause.* **Cissy** *pulls out her handkerchief.*

Here.

Verna *takes it. Blows her nose. She holds her head in her hands. Long pause.*

I'm not like 'im. I've tried to be. He never saw any bad in anybody. Never like upset, did he? Owt for a quiet life. He's still 'ere, you know. I don't mean I've seen 'im, but I know 'e's 'ere. (*Pause.*) He wouldn't want this, would he? (*Pause.*) Do you want a paracetamol?

The scene fades.

Scene Four

The same. Later.

Alma *and* **Verna** *are sitting on the porch.*

Verna   She couldn't see me?

Alma   No. (*Pause.*) What with that and her leg ... She fell off the cellar steps. Cut it. It went all weepy. She's got an' 'ome 'elp. I come round when I can.

Verna   She never even saw me.

Pause.

Alma   Somebody said to me once they'd seen you.

Verna   I don't go into town much. There's shops near. I'm in a council flat.

Alma   Oh. On your own?

Verna   I am now. Three years.

Alma   Were you ... married?

Verna   No.

Alma   Nobody since?

Verna   Not really. You, though. Seventeen years is it now, you and Earl?

Alma   Minus five week parole. I left 'im last year. Nobody else. Just 'im. 'Ad enough.

Verna   But you're OK now?

Alma   There's Neville ...

Verna   How is he?

Alma   Left school now.

Verna   Has he?

Alma   Starts work Monday. Garden Centre.

Verna   Oh. Not still wanting to be a farmer, then?

Alma   You remember?

Verna   That's all he ever wanted to do when he was little, wasn't it?

Alma   His first week of school, came home on the Friday and said he wasn't going back any more . . .

Verna   'It's all reading and writing. When are they going to do animals?'

A little laugh between them.

Alma   I don't know what's in his head any more.

Pause.

Verna   Danum's doing well, then.

Alma   It's doing ever so well. I work there.

Verna   Do you?

Alma   Full time now. It's always full of folk. Specially now, this time of year. You can't move.

Verna   I'll 'ave to go up, take a look.

Alma   You will. Just to see how it's all changed. You wouldn't know what it once was if you didn't know. Levelled. Slag 'eaps, everything. The only thing left to show what it was are six coal wagons. They've got them in the car park, full of flowers.

Pause.

Verna   Flowers.

Alma   Yes. (*Pause.*) Is JJ really the spit of Joe?

Verna   So I've been told this morning. Billy Winder. I met him up the cemetery.

Alma   Oh yes. (*Pause.*) Joe. The flowers. I –

Verna You?

Alma Whenever mam gets me to take some up to dad, I sneak one or two. I don't like to see it without.

Verna Thanks.

Pause.

Alma So JJ will be starting at big school in September?

Verna Yes.

Alma Is he looking forward to it?

Verna A bit scared.

Alma Aah. All in his new uniform.

Verna I've got to get it yet.

Alma It all goes so quick, doesn't it? You wish you could hang on to it sometimes. I say to Earl, there'll come a day you wish you had spent more time with him, and that'll be the day you realize it's too late. He's gone. Grown up and away.

Verna Are things OK with you, Alma?

Alma Are you and JJ close?

Verna Yes.

Alma I suppose you're bound to be.

Verna Do you want to meet him tomorrow?

Alma I'd love to.

Verna Well we'll do that, then.

Alma I'm at work, though.

Verna Well maybe we'll take a walk up to see you.

Alma I get a break in the afternoon. Half two. Ten minutes. There's a tea-room.

Verna Full of hanging baskets.

Alma Have you been?

Verna No. That's how I see it.

Alma It is. And all the tables have little pots of chrysanths. They look lovely. Mind you I never liked the smell. (*Pause.*) Were you really in hospital?

Verna You think I'd make that up?

Alma I'm sorry.

Verna Hysterectomy.

Alma Oh.

Verna I'm all right now. I 'ope. I was probably upstairs while you were downstairs with dad.

Alma You think?

Verna Maybe.

Alma No. You would have known.

Verna How?

Alma No. Nothing.

Verna Come on, tell me.

Alma If you were there, you would have felt me sending messages.

Verna Did you?

Alma Yes.

Pause.

Verna 'Where are you when I need you, you selfish bitch!'

Alma You WERE upstairs!

They laugh a little. **Neville** *arrives.*

Talk of the devil.

Verna It never is.

Alma It is.

Verna Now then.

Alma This is your Aunty Verna. Do you remember her?

Neville *gives her a little smile.*

Neville (*to* **Alma**) My dad says what's happenin' about tea?

Alma Get yourselves fish and chips.

Neville Right. (*He begins to move off.*)

Alma Neville. (*He stops. She takes out a fiver. He comes back for it.*) Just say hello, will you?

Neville (*to* **Verna**) All right?

Alma She won't bite.

Neville You took us to the cinema once.

Verna I did.

Neville *The Goonies.*

Verna You remember.

Neville Yea. See you. (*Moves off.*)

Alma Tell 'im I'll be 'ome in a bit.

Neville Do you want owt fetchin'?

Alma No, thanks.

He goes.

I'm sorry about Earl.

Verna It's all right.

Alma I know, but there's no need for ignorance. What's done is done.

Verna Is it?

Alma Eh?

Verna What's done?

Alma Well, twelve years. If you can't forgive and forget . . .

Verna What?

Alma Still being like they are. I mean. What's the use of that? Everybody told them at the time, everybody said it were only grief talking, you didn't mean any of it. You should 'ave 'eard mam when dad died. Weeks we 'ad it. The hate that came out of her mouth. For everybody. If I'd 'ave believed any of it, I'd 'ave never spoke to her again. But you don't let yourself believe it. You learn to know it's only grief talking. I suppose them two, because Joe was a mate, what you said to them . . . Pride gets in the way of a lot of things wi' men, doesn't it? Do you think? That's what I think it must be, don't you?

Verna Grief talking.

Alma Yes.

Verna Everybody told 'em that's what it was.

Alma Yes.

Verna But they wouldn't forgive? Still won't?

Alma I'm just saying. It must be that.

Verna Must it?

Alma What?

Verna That's what took 'em out of 'ere tonight wi'out a word?

Alma I didn't mean to upset you. I'm just trying to understand it. (*Pause.*) What, then? Verna? What else is it? Tell me. Tell me what it is, then.

Verna I don't know.

Alma I want to know what you think it is. Say it. (*Pause.*) What have you come back for Verna? To say it all over again?

Verna I've come back for Joe. And to see my sister and my mother.

Alma You still believe what you said back then, don't you?

Verna I haven't come back for this, Alma.

Alma But it's still there.

Verna Yes. Look, please, Alma, don't –

Alma Do you know who's put up most of the money for this memorial stone? When it looked like they weren't going to raise enough for it?

Verna Danum?

Alma You've got him to thank that Sunday's 'appenin' at all.

Verna Danum's paid for it?

Alma Yes. Because Joe was a friend. Like the others were friends. Out of respect and honour for what they stood for.

Verna Don't tell me this.

Alma I'm telling you. That's your brother. Comin' back 'ere with all that still in your head. What are you at? An accident. It was an accident. You lost Joe. Why – why can't you accept that? Why do you still want to blame somebody. Your own family? What kind of a woman are you to do that? What are you? They're right. You're not worth it. You're not worth it. There's something wrong with you, Verna. I mean it. You lost the man you loved, you look at your son every day and you see him and you can't let go. You're still wanting vengeance on somebody. Your own family. You see me and mine and when I tell you things aren't so good it – it makes you feel a bit better. You're sick. How can you be like this? The sister I had went away. She never came back.

Verna The sister you had went away telling you exactly what she's telling you now. Danum knew it was going to happen.

Alma He didn't know. He didn't know. He thought maybe – maybe something might happen –

Verna It did.

Alma Not the way he said it would. He said they'd come round to your house. He never said about the pit. He never said about once they were down the pit because he didn't know. It was an accident. They were all picked volunteers doing a safety check. Nobody even knew who they were, they –

Verna He knew! There wasn't a man even dreamt of working Danum didn't know about.

Alma He wasn't involved in any of it, though.

Verna Oh, Alma, he was up to his neck in it. They both were, him and Earl.

Alma Stop it! I'm not listening to any more of this.

Verna You asked me. I didn't want this!

Alma I just thought – I thought –

Verna Yea, well we know what thought did.

Alma I've been wrong about you.

Verna Looks like.

Alma *makes to go.*

Mam knew. The night Billy Winder got bust up.

Alma Knew what?

Verna Who was behind it. (*Pause.*) Danum and Earl.

Alma It was them?

Verna No. They got somebody else to do their dirty work.

Alma Mam knows? How? What happened? Verna?

The scene changes. The yard. Late night. Twelve years ago.
Danum *comes out of the house drinking tea from a mug.*

Danum   Come on in.

Verna   No, I'm all right.

Danum   It's all over now. There's nowt to see. I've made a pot of tea.

Verna   I'll wait for mam and dad.

Danum   Mam'll still be yappin' about it. (*Pause.*) He'll be all right. Looks worse than it is.

Verna   He looks dead.

Danum   He's not dead.

Verna   I thought it was my dad.

Danum   I know. I know. (*Pause.*) I wondered what the 'ell were up when you spotted us walking across. Running at 'im. 'Uggin and crying all over 'im.

Verna   We both thought it was 'im. We were sat 'ere. Heard the commotion. My heart just went . . .

Danum   You knew we were in 'welfare.

Verna   I know. I knew he was with you. I just suddenly felt something had happened to him. We thought there'd been an accident. A car or something. Even when I saw him, stood over him, I still thought it was dad. His face. You couldn't even make out who it was.

Danum   Leave it, Verna. That's it now. No use dwellin'. It's done now. He'll be all right. He's a tough old boot.

Verna   They kicked him senseless. He's nigh on fifty. What has he ever done to anybody? I hope they find whoever it was and pull their –

Danum   They're long gone.

Cissy *arrives from the yard end.*

Cissy (*to* **Verna**)   Ambulance 'as teken 'im. Your dad's gone with 'im.

Verna Is he going to be all right?

Cissy He's alive.

Verna What have they done it for? What's Billy ever done?

Cissy Never a bad word for anybody, that man.

Verna He's not a scab. He wouldn't do that. Would he?

Cissy No. You don't 'ave to be, lately. Just think about it is enough. Let anybody know you're 'avin second thoughts and they're round.

Verna You think that's it? Danum?

Danum Dunno.

Cissy *looks at him.*

Danum What? I know nowt about it. I don't know what he's said, what he's done.

Cissy Don't you?

Danum What you on about?

Cissy He keeps himself to himself, doesn't he?

Danum I don't know. Yea, I suppose.

Cissy No suppose about it. But he talked to your dad, didn't he?

Danum Eh? When?

Cissy Other day. The day your dad asked you what it was all about.

Danum Eh?

Cissy Your dad said to you Billy had had words with 'im. I were in 'kitchen. I 'eard you.

Danum Yea? So?

Cissy He told you that Billy said he'd seen you. Seen

you and Earl wi' two blokes. Sat talking in a car up Common Lane end.

Danum   Yea?

Cissy   And you said Billy must be blind. It wasn't you.

Danum   It wa'nt.

Cissy   But not so blind he couldn't tell your dad who they were.

Danum   It weren't me with 'em.

Cissy   No. He recognized two blokes he'd seen just once before. Handin' out pick axe 'andles from 'boot of their bloody car at Markham Main. He recognized them. But not you, who he's known all his life. Not Earl.

Danum   I've told you, it weren't me.

Cissy   Don't lie to me. I'm your mother.

Danum   Jesus! I'm not lying!

Cissy (*swiping him across the face*)   Don't you call up his name to help you!

Verna   Mam.

Cissy   I know. All right? I can put two and two together. And your father'll make four soon enough.

Danum   You're mad. He'd better not bloody say owt. I've nowt to do wi' this. What's he gunna do?

Cissy   What's he gunna do? I know what he ought to do. What do you think he's gunna do? What CAN he do, eh? What CAN he do? Keep his bloody mouth shut, that's what he'll do for you. Keep his mouth shut. (*To* **Verna**.) And you do 'same.

Danum   I ant done owt!

Cissy   Just bugger off, Danum. Just go, will you? Before I say summat I will regret.

Danum   Mam, just listen, you can't go round –

Cissy No. Don't talk to me. Just go.

He starts towards the house.

Not in there.

Danum What?

Cissy Go and stay at one of your girlfriends for the night. I don't want you 'ere tonight. I don't want you 'ere when your dad gets back. I'll talk to 'im. You're his son, he's not going to talk. Get yoursen gone. Go.

Danum *moves off.* **Cissy** *turns to go in.*

Verna Mam . . .

Cissy *turns to her.*

Cissy Not one word. Ever.

She turns back. Goes in. The lights change back.

Alma They both knew? Mam and dad?

Verna Yes. And the one that's left that knows, you can't ask. Don't ever ask her, Alma. (*Pause.*) I'm not saying Earl was in on everything, organizing it all. I don't think he was. That was Danum. Earl was the chauffeur. That's all.

Alma He must have known what was going on? (*Pause.*) But Joe. Joe! You can't say that, Verna, you know you can't. I won't let you say that.

Verna Alma, all time and turning it over has done for me is burn me up inside, not really knowing what happened, not being able to do anything about it, not wanting to, most days. Most days I'm just plain lonely for what I've lost — not just Joe — you, mam . . . This place. I wanted this — this week-end to try, to make something . . . I can't help what's in here, Alma. I want it to be OK. Really. I do. But I can't be blind to the pieces I see. They nag. You tell me Danum put up the money for this and in my head I know it's a good thing. But something makes me sick at what it could be.

Alma   What? What?

Verna   I can't − I don't want to make it into a word.

Alma   Do you hate him?

Verna   No. No, not hate.

Alma   What, then?

Verna   I can't hate somebody I don't know. It's not knowing, guessing, having just pieces of it . . .

Alma   And if you had them all? And it fitted together to show that it was him? What then? What would you do?

Pause.

Verna   What would you do?

Act Two – Saturday

Scene One

Late morning

Cissy *and* **Neville** *are sitting on the porch.*

Cissy   When you think o' that slag, and all what's growin' on it now ... all them plants, all that colour. You see, that's what people want. Bit o' nature in their own back yard. If 'rest 'o 'world's bein' buggered up, at least you can sit in your own back yard and mek do wi'that. Make it nice.

Neville   Is that what you're doin' 'ere, then?

Cissy   Your mam's idea. Brighten it up a bit. It'd be nice if I could see it. Is it nice?

Neville   Yea.

Cissy   Smells nice. (*Pause.*) She allus did like flowers. Used to bring 'em 'ome as a kid – wild flowers, like. Only she'd just bring 'eads – no stalks. We could never get it through to 'er you needed 'stalks an' all. So we 'ad to set to and fill a bowl wi' water and float flower 'eads on it. She thought it looked lovely. We 'ad 'em on 'sideboard. Folk used to think it looked a bit queer but we got used to it. She'd get up in a morning, stir 'em round with 'er finger to make a different pattern for the day. She 'ad some funny ideas as a kid.

Pause.

Neville   Were me Aunty Verna 'same?

Cissy   Eh? No. Chalk and cheese, them two. (*Smiling.*) Verna were allus a mardy little bugger, nowt'd please 'er. 'Ave you seen 'er, then?

Neville   Last night.

Cissy   Oh. What did she say?

Neville Nowt. Seems all right. I don't remember her much.

Cissy No, you wouldn't. What were you – four?

Neville Yea, mebbe.

Cissy Not much more.

Pause.

Neville Were this bloke 'er 'usband?

Cissy Joe? I think it were on 'cards, like. She were expectin'.

Pause.

Neville They've got 'handstand up.

Cissy 'Ave they?

Neville They were puttin' up some flags on strings.

Cissy Oh aye?

Pause.

Neville Me dad dunt like 'er much.

Cissy No? What's he say, then?

Neville 'E dunt like 'idea of me mam gettin' back in wi' 'er. They 'ad a row about it last night.

Cissy Did they?

Neville I went upstairs. I 'ad to put me stereo on. Me dad slammed out in 'finish.

Pause.

Cissy Well they were close when they were younger.

Neville Who?

Cissy Your mam and Verna.

Neville Were they?

Cissy Very close – apart from when they weren't

clobberin' one another. (*Pause.*) Your mam's missed 'er, I suppose.

Neville   Yea.

Cissy   Verna were allus 'strongest o' two of 'em. I mean standin' up for herself. Your mam's allus bin a bit on 'vulnerable side, allus gettin' 'erself in a state over summat or other. Verna'd be forever 'avin to sort out somebody in 'playground for 'avin a go at 'er sister.

Neville   Dint me uncle Danum do that?

Cissy   He were in 'big school by then.

Neville   I wunt mind a brother.

Cissy   It dunt allus 'appen they get on. I know families where they've 'ated one another. And I mean 'ate. Real 'ate. Live in 'same street but cross it sooner than 'ave to walk past their own family.

Neville   Yea, but that were all to do wi' strike, weren't it? (*Pause.*) Is that why she left?

Cissy   Who told you that?

Neville   Is that why she ant bin back?

Cissy   Who's told you this?

Neville   'S what I got from last night.

Cissy   Well it weren't.

Pause.

Neville   Did you kick 'er out 'cos she were expectin'?

Cissy   Don't be so bloody cheeky. No I didn't. She weren't livin' 'ere.

Neville   I'm only askin'.

Cissy   What a thing to say. She just left. People do, you know.

Neville   I know.

Pause.

Cissy You got that bloody daft idea o' goin' in 'army out your 'ead yet?

Neville Yea.

Cissy Thank God for that. Your mother 'd 've 'ad a fit if she'd known. Any silly bugger can go and get 'imself shot. If your great grandad were 'ere 'e'd tell you.

Pause.

Neville Yea. Well he's not.

Cissy No. (*She takes out a tissue, wipes her eyes. Pause.*) Will you go to 'shop and get me some liquorice torpedoes?

Neville I've got to go up 'allotments. I said I'd water Billy's while he's at work. I'll get you some. Bring 'em round later.

Cissy 'Ere, then, fetch me me purse.

Neville No, I've got some money. You give me some yesterday.

Cissy That were for you.

Neville I've got some money.

Cissy If they ant got any o' them, I'll 'ave a quarter of gum drops.

Neville Eh?

Cissy Wine gums.

Neville Right. I'll see you, then.

He goes. **Cissy** *closes her eyes, sleeps. The scene fades.*

Scene Two

Mid-day

Cissy *as before.* **Alma** *comes out of the house in her 'uniform',* *with a drink for* **Cissy**.

Cissy There's only one cause for an 'isterectomy at 'er age.

Alma What's that? (*She hands* **Cissy** *the drink.*)

Cissy I'm gettin' to quite like this stuff. It's not bad, is it?

Alma No.

Cissy Too much of the other.

Alma What? Don't be daft.

Cissy I'm tellin' you. That lass o' Spinks' 'ad one in her thirties. 'Er 'usband could never leave 'er alone. 'Er mother told me. She walked about like a ghost, poor lass.

Alma Verna's not got an 'usband.

Cissy No. And do you wonder why?

Alma No. Why?

Cissy Think about it.

Alma I am.

Cissy Who's going to want to marry 'er with a kid twelve year old? All they're wanting is a bit on the side.

Alma And you're saying she gives it to 'em, are you?

Cissy Don't be so vulgar. I'm saying. If she wants a bloke bad enough . . .

Alma She doesn't.

Cissy Aye. She might tell you that. I can 'ear it be'ind 'er voice.

Alma What?

Cissy Lonely for a bit o' love.

Alma Is she?

Cissy Blokes like that, you see, think to themselves, 'Aye

aye, this is a pushover.' I know. I'm not daft. I weren't born yesterday. I bet she'd need her fingers AND toes to tot up the number of blokes who's telled 'er they love 'er just to get 'er in bed and then bugger off, never to set foot over 'doorstep again.

Alma   I don't think so.

Pause.

Cissy   She's never going to find another Joe, I know that.

Alma   No.

Cissy   She did love 'im, didn't she? (*Pause.*) That's one thing I DO know. I don't think I've ever seen anybody so much in love. She were 'alf barmy with it. (*Pause.*) You were never like that.

Alma   No. (*Pause.*) Were you?

Cissy   Me? Well I loved 'im. I didn't parade it round 'streets if that's what you mean.

Alma   I didn't mean that.

Cissy   You couldn't anyway, not in them days. Only sort of women that did were thought – well, tarts. (*Pause.*) I didn't mean – when I said you were never in love like that, I didn't mean you weren't in love. What I meant was, well you knew Earl from school, didn't you? It were all . . . from friends, knockin' about together.

Alma   You mean it were a foregone conclusion we'd get wed.

Cissy   No.

Alma   It were. Might as well. Summat to do.

Cissy   Don't say that. You know that's not it. You're only saying that 'cos you're finding fault, you've 'ad another set to and you're wantin' to unravel it to see where you went wrong. You didn't. Every couple 'as their ups and downs, Alma. It'd be a bit queer if they didn't. Me and your dad were allus rowin'. It never meant owt. You 'ave to stick with it, for better or worse.

Alma Yea? Well that makes for a fine prospect.

Cissy What were it about then?

Alma What?

Cissy Last night?

Alma I've told you. Verna.

Cissy He's just jealous that she's 'ere. She's somebody what knows a part of your life that he doesn't. Some folk can't abide the thought of that. He dunt want to share you wi' anybody, that's all. It's jealousy.

Alma Yea. And there's a part of 'is life I never knew owt about . . . but I'm learning.

Cissy What do you mean?

Alma What I'm learning I don't like.

Cissy What?

Alma Not about before I met 'im. I mean while I've bin married to 'im.

Cissy What? Is he . . .?

Alma Who'd 'ave 'im? They're welcome to 'im.

Cissy You're gettin' very bitter as you get older, you are. I don't know who the 'ell you tek after. What do you mean, then, if it's not another woman?

Alma Did you know dad?

Cissy What do you mean? I 'ope so.

Alma I mean REALLY know 'im.

Cissy Course I knew 'im. He never looked at another woman in 'is life.

Alma I don't mean that. I mean . . . you know what I

mean.

Cissy Did I trust 'im? Did he ever lie?

Alma Not about women – was he really, inside, the person you saw?

Cissy We're gettin' quite philosophical all of a sudden, aren't we?

Alma Was 'e?

Cissy 'Ow the bloody 'ell should I know? (*She shifts about in her chair.*) I know I 'ad a bloody awful night on that bed. It's facing the wrong way. I'm used to sleeping east-west. You've put me north-south.

Alma It were the only way it'd go in 'front room.

Cissy And being downstairs I 'ad to shut 'curtains when I like 'em open. I didn't sleep a wink. Felt like I'd bin run over by a bus this morning.

Alma You're not used to it, that's all. It's with it being a single.

Cissy Then when I finally did drop off I 'ad the daftest dream.

Alma What about?

Cissy I were pushing you and Verna 'ome in an Asda trolley wi' all me shoppin', and we kept getting stuck in ruts in the road. And I looked down and this crack opened up and your dad were there in his pit gear and I said, 'I've got you a nice bit o' mackerel for your tea.' (*Pause.*) You dream the daftest things. I wonder what it means? I wondered where the 'ell I was when I did wake up. Took me ten minutes to get me bearings. I thought I'd died and wok up in a funeral parlour. (*Pause.*) I sometimes wake up, even now, and expect 'im to be laid at 'side o' me. I think, 'oh, he must 'ave got up and gone down to 'ave a fag and make himself a cup o' tea.' Even calling him sometimes. 'Frank? Are you there?' And I swear I can smell bacon

frying and fag smoke drifting up the stairs. Some mornings
I must be five or ten minutes lying there, before it dawns
on me 'e's dead. It's as if your mind gets stuck in what
were. I mean, thirty-nine years of it. Your mind must fix
itself in that – what was, what you thought then 'd be
forever, what you took for granted, I suppose.

Alma I sometimes think of Neville still at juniors, and 'is
it cubs night tonight?' Sometimes I wake up fourteen again
. . . must be something you dream, but I can wake up and
think, 'Is it Saturday? Is it a school day?' and for a second,
Earl is . . . who's this in my bed?

Neville *arrives.*

Neville Billy Winder's allotment's been wrecked.

Alma Eh?

Neville Somebody's been and pulled the lot up, just
chucked it all over.

Cissy They 'aven't.

Neville Couple of other 'allotments, same.

Cissy What for?

Neville Some kids'll 've done it for a laugh. I've bin
trying to square it up.

Cissy Fancy.

Neville Can't save much, though. I've just piled up stuff.
Some on it might be all right.

Cissy The bloody little sods.

Neville Some bloke thought it were me.

Cissy What did you say?

Neville I said it weren't, like. I said I were just clearing
it up.

Cissy What did he say?

Neville He told me to eff off. Billy'll be well sick. (*To* **Alma**.) I thought I'd catch you so you can tell 'im at work.

Alma Yes. Yes, I'd better get off.

Alma *picks up* **Cissy**'s *glass, takes it in.*

Neville Here's your spice. (*He hands her the bag of sweets.*)

Cissy Oh, thanks, love. You're a good lad. I don't know, what's in their 'eads these days to do a thing like that? You can 'ave nowt. They'll a bin out last night, roamin' about looking for mischief.

Alma *comes out.*

I blame 'parents.

Alma I'll get off, then.

Cissy All that work, all them hours he's put in.

Neville (*to* **Cissy**) You got any dustbin liners or owt I can put some stuff in?

Alma Are you going back?

Neville Yea.

Cissy Aye, and if that nosey bugger says owt, you just tell 'im from me to 'eff off 'isself.

Neville Right.

Cissy There's some under 'sink.

Neville (*to* **Alma**) I just wanna get it squared up a bit.

Alma Thanks, Neville. Good lad.

Neville *goes in.*

Cissy He's a good lad.

Alma Yes. I'll see you Mum.

Cissy Rather you than me.

Alma Eh?

Cissy   Tellin' 'im.

Alma   What?

Cissy   Billy.

Alma   I know. Bye.

Cissy   Bye, love. Eh. (**Alma** *stops.*) Earl. It's nowt. He's your 'usband. Think on.

Alma   I am.

Neville *comes out with bin liners.*

Neville   See you.

Alma *smiles at him, goes.*

Cissy   You found 'em?

Neville   Yea.

Cissy   How many you got?

Neville   Couple.

Cissy   Tek what you want, there's plenty.

Neville   These'll do. (*He moves down into the yard.*)

Cissy   'As he got any broad beans this year? If he 'as, I'll 'ave some.

Neville   What do they look like?

Cissy   Never mind.

Neville   See you.

Cissy   Aye.

He goes.

Nice wi' a bit o' gammon. Not that I've got any o' that, either.

She opens the sweet bag, takes out a couple of torpedoes. Eats them. The scene fades.

Scene Three

Early evening

Billy *is stood in the yard, some way from* **Alma** *and* **Verna** *who are sat on the porch step.*

Billy Can I go now? Tha's got some front, I'll say that. (*To* **Alma**.) 'Cos you THINK Earl did it, after a row wi' you, digging up what's long dead, you want me to an' all? There's nowt to dig up.

Alma I've told you, I saw you this morning, Billy.

Billy And I've told you, he were askin' me about 'job, how I were gettin' on wi' it.

Alma Danum wouldn't give you the time of day.

Billy Oh, you know 'ow I am wi' 'im, do you?

Alma He never has the time of day for anybody, less they're in a mini skirt. What is there to ask about parking cars? He were warning you off.

Billy Look, I've nowt to tell yer. What you trying to do? Eh? What's it gunna do to thi mother if she gets wind?

Alma She won't.

Billy Your mother gets downwind of a bit o' scandal, she can smell it before anybody's put words to it. (*Pause.*) I don't know if it were Danum set somebody on me that night. Just for seeing him wi' a couple of hoodlums? You say it wor. That's for you to think if tha wants to. I knew nowt then, and I've learnt nowt since. It 'appened, I gor over it. I'm still 'ere.

Verna Yes, you're still 'ere.

Billy What?

Verna Go home, Billy, if your conscience is clear. Go home.

Billy Wh – Me? What 'ave I done? Eh? What 'ave I

done?

Verna Grown old.

Billy What's that supposed to mean?

Verna We shouldn't 'ave asked you about it. I'm sorry. We shouldn't 'ave. It was a mistake. I was mistaken, that's all.

Billy What do you mean, 'grown old'? You cheeky bugger.

Verna I'm sorry.

Billy Tha's said it now. Come on.

Verna We've all grown old. It's too late. It's too late. If ever we did have a chance of something – something decent – we blew it long ago.

Verna *is suddenly tearful.* **Billy** *starts to move off.*

(*To herself.*) Self respect. Where did that end up, eh?

Billy *stops, turns on her.*

Billy You talking to me?

Verna Me. I'm talking to me! What did I do for Joe but forget him, forget me, and – A one man woman. Me? Once upon a time. Once –

Billy Shut up, Verna.

Verna What you'll do for any man when you've lost your self.

Billy Aye, all right. That'll do.

Verna Respect. When I let him go. When I said 'So what? What can I do?' It wasn't an accident, but who am I to say? Leave it, don't fight, forget. Forget what was the only thing keeping me going. How do you do that? If you lie down and lie to yourself enough . . .

Billy You've a son. His son. Isn't he worth – ?

Verna Oh, he's fine. His dad's a hero. Fighting for a cause. Died in a pit accident, risked his life so that a pit wouldn't die. Proud day, Sunday.

Billy Aye. He should –

Verna An accident that wasn't. A pit that was never going to open again. A bloody garden centre with flowers in the coal wagons! Oh, I can let him live a lie. I've done it for twelve year, I can do it for another twelve.

Billy What Joe did, what he was, wasn't a lie.

Verna His death was a lie! I know it and you know it. You KNOW it, Billy, and we're still keeping that lie alive. Yes, my son can live with a lie if he never knows it is. No, only me, Billy, only me that rots away from the inside. You? You always were a tough old boot. Bounced off. You never even let it in, did you? Did you? (*Pause.*) It's OK, Billy. I'm not ... You know something? I'm willing to bet there's more than me and you know what's gone on. They're out there and know what's what. I wouldn't be surprised if 'alf of 'village knows. And THAT'S what's so ... sad? It's not for me to come back and haunt them – they're already dead to it. Time's moved on and turned it all upside down. Danum is the hero of this place. I saw that this afternoon; what he's done, jobs he's provided, folks he's seen all right, 'elped out. Am I right? (*Pause.*) Go home, Billy, it's too late.

Billy There's nowt nobody can do about any of it. How many years do you wait, for the day when things'll be set right? Not in my lifetime. Not in yours. You 'ave all on just to keep goin'. You go blind to stuff. Who's not on some bloody scam or other? If you're on 'dole you've got to. Them in work know they're bloody lucky for as long as it lasts.

Aye, I've grown old, lass. Could you ever imagine a bolshy bugger like me parking cars in a garden centre for a pittance? On that pit top where I worked twenty odd year, where me dad worked all his life? Even my name. Me dad were Ted the Winder – that were his job – fetchin' cage up and down all day – Ted the Winder, not Ted Jessop, not Billy Jessop – did you know that were my name? 'Anded down from me dad's job to me. Now 'is lad is walkin' round in 'wind and rain, every five minutes somebody tellin' me what to do, when to 'ave a piss. Supervisors – blokes I've worked alongside, shown 'em 'ow to go on wi' job, now they're tellin' me. Do I say owt? When you live to eat, you don't buck. You keep your 'ead down.

Alma And what do you do when the bit of stuff you grow yoursen, to eat, to sell on, all goes in one night?

Billy You start again.

Verna I loved the people in this place.

Billy You can't turn it back, lass. None of it.

Alma Somebody thinks YOU can. Earl thinks you can.

Billy It weren't 'im!

Alma It were! He knows you can turn it back if you want to, he knows you're a danger to 'im over what went on. He knows you've something on the pair of 'em. What? It were probably Danum told 'im to do the bloody job. Can't you see that? He probably went straight out of our 'ouse round to 'phone box to tell 'im.

Billy Why did you 'ave to bring me into it?

Alma Are you frightened of what they might still do?

Cissy *comes out.*

Cissy Is who frightened of what?

Billy Cissy.

Cissy Oh, it's you, Billy. What's all 'commotion in aid of?

Verna Hello, Mam.

Cissy Verna? What's gone on?

Verna Nothing.

Cissy (*to* **Alma**) You telled 'im?

Alma Yes.

Billy Aye. I've been up and seen. You've a bag full o' veg 'ere, to share out between you.

Cissy Oh, Billy, you shouldn't 'ave.

Billy It waint keep.

Cissy Our Neville's been all day trying to square up.

Billy I saw 'im.

Cissy He were 'eartbroke about it. Weren't he?

Alma Yes.

Cissy Little bleeders. (*Pause.*) What you frightened of, they might come back and 'ave another go when you've got it all going again?

Billy Aye.

Cissy You want to get yourself a shot gun. Pepper their arses for 'em. I would. Teach the buggers a lesson. (*To* **Verna**.) You see what it's like round 'ere now? This is what we 'ave to put up with these days. Bloody kids wi' nowt better to do than go round givin' other folk trouble. And if you say owt they just laugh at you. That there memorial won't last five minutes. You see if I'm right. Where it is, that's where they all meet up in their gang. It'll be covered in bloody spray paint in no time. No respect for nowt nor nobody.

Alma It wasn't kids.

Verna Alma!

Alma I want to know! I want to know this! Don't you?

Billy *makes a move to go.*

Verna Not this way.

Cissy What the 'ell's goin' on?

Alma Billy. Don't! Don't walk away from it. Just –
Nobody's going to DO anything. Billy! (*He stops.*) None of
us are – We just want to understand it. We're not out to
put things right – we can't, we all know that. Don't I
deserve to know something about my 'usband? Doesn't
Verna deserve to know something? Just to know, that's all.
We're not taking it outside this yard. We're not. (*To*
Verna.) Tell him you're not. Verna!

Cissy Will somebody tell me what's going on?

Alma Verna!

Verna *just looks at* **Billy**, *who meets her eyes.*

Cissy Tell me!

Alma (*to* **Cissy**) It was Earl!

Billy (*to* **Verna**) You think what you want o' me, lass.
I'm going. Not for me. (*Pointing at* **Cissy**.) For her. For
your mother. (*He makes to go.*)

Cissy Billy. Billy!

He stops, turns to her.

Billy Don't, Cissy.

Cissy Just wait a minute. (*To* **Alma**.) Earl?

Alma (*looking at* **Billy**) Yes.

Cissy (*to* **Verna**) You told her about Billy?

Verna *can't speak.*

Billy (*suddenly realizing, to* **Cissy**) You knew?

Cissy (*to* **Alma**) And this is what you rowed about last
night?

Alma Yes.

Billy Cissy. You knew what they – ? You knew they
were behind what 'appened to me?

Cissy Could I 'ave said it to you? What were I supposed to do? My own son?

Billy I know. I know that. I just wish you 'adn't known.

Cissy Aye. Wishes and 'opes.

Billy I'm sorry.

Cissy So am I. (*Pause. To* **Verna**.) You've started summat now, aven't you? Are you satisfied?

The scene fades.

Scene Four

The yard, later that night.

Verna *is sitting on the porch.* **Earl** *arrives, striding up the yard.*

Verna Don't, Earl, mam's not too good.

Earl What's up wi' 'er?

Verna Alma'll be out in a minute.

Earl Might as well bloody live 'ere. What's up wi' er?

Verna Just a dizzy spell. She'll be all right.

Earl 'As tha seen Neville?

Verna Can't you make your own tea?

Earl Tell 'er I'm up 'welfare.

Verna He's gone to the pictures with my lad. Billy Winder give 'em both a couple o' quid for clearing up 'is allotment.

Earl Tell 'er I'll get summat to eat up there.

Verna OK. Will you put this in your van? (*She picks up the bin liner of veg.*) Alma can't carry it 'ome.

Earl What is it?

Verna Leftovers.

He takes the bag, looks in.

You never were very bright, were you?

Earl You what?

Verna It weren't exactly 'ard to work out.

Earl What?

Verna Who it was.

Earl Eh?

Verna Did Danum tell you to do it?

Earl What you on about?

Verna He used you then, he's using you now.

Earl Eh?

Verna He's always used you, Earl.

Earl No 'e ant.

Verna Because he knew you weren't bright enough to see through what he were doing.

Earl Sod off.

Verna You'd like me to, wouldn't you?

Earl Yes. I would.

Verna Why? Why do I worry you, Earl?

Earl You?

Verna Me.

Earl You don't. You're just a shit stirrer.

Alma *comes out.*

You put ideas in 'er 'ead about things.

Verna What things? What kind of person you really are?

Earl (*to* **Alma**) You bloody livin' 'ere now or what? Only I'd like to know what's 'appenin, you know? Be nice now and then to come 'ome and there be somebody in.

Alma   Would it?

Earl   What?

Alma   To run around after you?

Earl (*to* **Verna**)   You see? This is what I'm on about. (*To* **Alma**.) Well you can bloody well stop as long as you want, I'm off out.

Alma   Thank you. I didn't realize I 'ad to 'ave your permission.

Earl   Oh. (*To* **Verna**.) Ant tekken you long, 'as it?

Verna   You tekkin' that bag or what?

Alma   What you given 'im it for?

Earl   Shove it up your arse! (*He throws it at them, turns to go.*)

Verna   You go near Billy Winder again and I'll tell everything I know!

He turns back. **Alma** *looks at* **Verna**.

I mean it.

Earl (*to* **Alma**)   She's bloody mental. There's summat the matter with 'er. Tell who what?

Alma   Verna, you said –

Verna   I lied.

Earl (*to* **Alma**)   For Christ's sake, what's she on with? (*To* **Verna**.) What are you saying? (*To* **Alma**.) Are you in this an' all, or what? Alma?

Alma *can't speak.*

Jesus. What the 'ell are you both playin' at now? (*To* **Verna**.) You've got some bloody gall to come back 'ere rakin' all this up. Nobody listened to your ravin' then and they won't now. You go to the bloody police. You do it.

Go on, see where it gets you. They'll bloody lock you up for bein' round the twist! How could I 'ave 'ad summat to do with it when I never went near?

Verna   So why does Billy Winder have to be shut up?

Earl   I don't know. Does he?

Verna   You do know! So he never tells anybody about who those two blokes really were!

Earl   What blokes?

Verna   Why was it so important to keep him quiet? Eh? Well we know now. We know. You thought 'ed be out of action till you'd done what you were plannin' that day. You didn't reckon on 'im bein' out in three week, back on that picket line in four. Did you? There on the gates the day those forty-seven volunteers came through in the coach – two of 'em he saw in the back of your car that day. He saw 'em, Earl. He saw 'em on that coach.

Earl   Yea? So? So what?

Verna   Are you telling me you knew they went down?

Earl   I don't know what the fuck you're on about.

Verna   You tellin' me you just drove Danum about and let 'im do all 'talking

Earl   He never did nowt.

Verna   While you sat there and shut your ears?

Earl   You've lost me.

Verna   They were thugs! You got to Billy 'cos he'd seen you with 'em. I know. Mam knows. Danum knows we know. All right? So don't try and come the wide-eyed bloody innocent! You tried to stop that safety check.

Earl   What?

Verna   And it worked, the first one you stopped. Got 'em to change their minds. Delayed it. But you knew they'd 'ave to go down sooner or later if that pit was goin' to be worked again. You couldn't stop it twice. So forty-seven blokes went down, knowin' by now it were gunna be dangerous. And two of 'em your men. Why?

Earl (*to* **Alma**)   Are you tekkin all this shit in?

Alma   If you can tell me different, no.

Earl   I 'ad nowt to do wi' what went on down that pit! I were trying to keep men away! I weren't going to give in and I 'elped make sure nobody else did either. Is that so wrong? Eh? (*To* **Alma**.) What you looking at me like that for?

Verna   And all the time you knew that pit were gettin' unsafe.

Earl   I didn't know that! I – we thought they'd give in, see sense, before it got too far gone.

Verna   But they didn't give in, did they? Why not?

Earl   'Cos the bastards were prepared to crush us even if it meant closin' 'pit. I know that now. I didn't then. Nobody did.

Verna   You thought a bit o' sabotage were gunna –

Earl   Now wait a minute, you can't –

Verna   – make coal board act quicker to get men back to work, to force 'em to agree to 'union's demands, and get blokes back?

Earl   I never 'ad nowt to do wi' sabotage. Don't you accuse me –

Verna   Why did them two go down then?

Earl   I don't know. I don't know!

Alma   Earl. I want to know if you knew those two men were in that party. Don't lie to me. Don't lie to me!

Earl   It were nowt to do with sabotage.
They were there to ... they were just gunna make sure that safety report read what they wanted it to read – get

'em all to agree to what were gunna be put down. If it
read worse than things wor, then 'board 'd act quicker to
get it all going again, wouldn't it? There were no sabotage.
They were down to fix that report not fix the pit. I'm
telling you.
Look. Alma. All Danum – all we did – our job were to let
certain blokes know who were startin' to cave in. That's all.
Then it were up to them. How they did it were nowt to
do wi' me.

Verna Turn a blind eye.

Earl Who do you think you are, eh?
For every bloke who finished up in 'ospital 'cos they
wouldn't be persuaded to see sense, there were twenty beat
up by 'police. You know. You saw it.

Verna I saw it. I saw your own friends put there by your
finger pointin' an all. And plenty of police.

Earl When a bastard stands there and deliberately taunts
you, calls you names, laughs at you, waves pound notes in
your face – they were gettin' 'undreds for that, for what
they were doin'. Overtime, danger money – and 'alf of 'em
weren't even police, just put in a uniform for 'day, drafted
in to 'ave a fight. You don't know the 'alf of it. I'll tell you
summat for nowt, to get your 'ead round, and it's not
rumour, it's fact. Some chief constable finished up wi' a
fuckin' yacht out of what he did. A thank you present from
this government. And do you know what the bastard called
it? 'Arthur Scargill'. A fucking yacht called Arthur Scargill
sailing the seas wi' that cunt smilin' all the way. Made
thousands. It cost 'government thousands to break us – but
that's what they were prepared to do – break us, I mean
break bloody 'eads, rather than let 'country see 'union win.
They caused that pit to get in the state it did. Not me.

Verna Why would they do that?

Earl I've just told you.

Verna Could it be they planned all along to close it?
Wanted it to shut down, and you gave 'em the chance?

Make it look like your fault not theirs?

Earl   Makes you wonder now.

Verna   It makes you wonder all right.
Earl, you were being used. You'd bin used all along. That
pit were planned to close months before, maybe even
before 'strike started. What those two blokes were doin' was
making sure, putting it out of action for good. Only it went
wrong. Something went wrong. Whatever they did took
them and three others with them. One of 'em Joe.

Earl   They will lock you up. None of us wanted that pit
to close.

Verna   Danum were working to shut it down.

Earl   Danum? Eh, now you are talking fucking balls. You
can just – There were nobody more rock solid than
Danum.

Verna   No?

Earl   No!

Verna   No, he didn't plan for five men to be killed. He
were probably doing what he did in the beginning for the
same reasons as you. But SOMEBODY, somebody got to
'im and told 'im what were goin' on, offered 'im a piece to
change sides. It were easy. All 'e 'ad to do were to carry
on keepin' blokes away from that pit as long as he could.
Till it were too late. He knew that pit was going to close.
He told me, Earl. He told me. He tried to get me to stop
Joe going down. He knew what were going to 'appen and
he knew the only way to stop Joe was if he told me to tell
'im it were all a waste of time. Nobody were gunna save
that pit. He knew. He were working for somebody in the
know for a piece of the pie. And he got it. Look what he
got for his services. Whose tender for that site was
accepted? Oh yes, he were clever enough to pool 'is
redundancy wi' four others – not you, though Earl, you
never even got a look in, did you? – but whose name was
it they saw? Who made sure he were lent the capital to set

it up?
You were used, Earl.

Earl Danum never knew. Nobody knew it were gunna
shut down. There's no way. He got that site fair and
square. There's no way on earth he were working for
them. Jesus, where do you get this?

Verna So why did he tell me the pit were finished?

Earl I don't know. Just trying to find a way to stop Joe —

Verna He was telling me what he knew.

Earl No. Just pack this in, will you? Pack it in! Where do
you get this crap, eh? You know this for a fact, eh? You
got some proof? (*Pause.*) No. I didn't think you 'ad. You've
got nothing 'cos there is nothing. How can you even think
that of 'im?

Verna You know what tomorrow's about?

Earl Eh?

Verna I think it's about covering his back.

Alma Don't say that, Verna.

Earl Is that what you think?

Verna Yes.

Earl Then I'm sorry for you. I am. If that's why you
think your brother put 'is 'and in 'is pocket. You think
honouring them men . . . he feels nothing about that?

Verna Oh yes, he feels something about that. What
about you, Earl, what do you feel?

Earl Sick. Knowin' my own sister-in-law is a fucking
witch.

Verna No, I've not got any proof of it, and I don't know
what I'd do with it if I had. But what I've got makes it all
fit, Earl.

Earl Not to me it doesn't.

Verna   Can he prove otherwise? 'Course he can. There'll be nothing. Nothing at all for anybody to prove a damn thing. But I know. That's enough. I know.

Earl   What you after, money?

Verna   I don't want his money!

Earl   What, then?

Verna   I want him to know I know. What he does with that . . . That's for him to work out for himself. No, I don't want him to admit to me what he's done. Is he ever going to do that? I just want him to know we've seen him for what he is. Alma, mam, know I'm not crazy with this. They know now there's something in it. I just want him to deny it to my face, to Alma, to my mother, to you – and then walk away and carry on with it, if he can.

Earl (*to* **Alma**)   Are you with her in this? Do you believe any of this? Eh? I'm talking to you!

Alma   I don't know. I don't know this about Danum.

Earl   Good. Some sense somewhere.

Alma   I know it was an accident that wouldn't have happened if you hadn't sent them men down – whatever you thought their job was.

Earl   So I'm to blame? Is that what you're saying? It was my fault? Danum set that up, not me.

Alma   And you've been covering for him ever since. Have you never felt in twelve years any kind of responsibility?

Earl   You don't say this to me. Do you hear? You don't say this to me! You're my wife!

Pause.

Verna   He was always the hero, wasn't he, Earl? You always looked up to him. Even when you were a raggy-arsed schoolkid knocking on our door for him to play. And it can never be wrong, whatever a hero gets you to do for them. It must be OK, because he's a great bloke, a pal.

Look at what he's achieved. He's used you, Earl, conned
you into thinking it was all for the good. There could
never be any bad in him or in what you did for him.
(*Pause.*) Was there any doubt? Ever? About what you did?

Pause.

Alma   Tell me there was, Earl. Tell me there was
something in there. Other than loyalty.

Earl   So loyalty means nothing any more, does it? It was
all you'd got. You looked after one another. That means
nothing now? Is that what you're saying? When everything
else goes – a way of life – you let that go too? What am I
if I do that? What am I to all the blokes I've worked with,
their fathers, and back as far as ever there was a pit? I
couldn't walk these streets, the cemetery, nowhere.
Whatever I've done, I've done for them. In their interest.
Always.

Verna   Even when five men die? Can you look at that
memorial tomorrow and still feel it was for the good of all?

Earl   What do you want from me? What do you want
from me?! You think I can tell you how I felt about that
day? You think I never felt owt? Is that what you're saying,
I felt nothing? You want the satisfaction of tellin' me your
grief was more terrible than anything I ever felt? You think
I don't know that? You think I don't know that however
bad I felt – numb for weeks, couldn't sit in, couldn't go
out, finding myself in a fuckin' field somewhere asking the
bloody trees for an answer – it was anywhere near what
you felt? What are you saying, I have nothing in 'ere to
grieve for your loss? (*Pause.*) Well fuck you! (*He turns and
strides off.*)

Alma   Earl. Earl!

Cissy (*from inside*)   Alma? Alma!

Alma *goes in the house.* **Verna** *sits on the porch. The scene fades.*

Act Three – Sunday

Scene One

Mid-morning.

Cissy *in her chair,* **Billy** *down in the yard,* **Alma** *sitting on the porch step.*

Cissy If you'd been asleep for days and wok up, you'd still know it were a Sunday. It 'as a feel to it, don't you think?
I allus thought so. Like you're waiting for summat to 'appen. They're a waiting day. The air's different. 'Eavier. Whenever I 'ad an 'eadache I allus knew what day it wor.

Alma Waiting for work on Monday.

Cissy Aye.

Billy You 'ad to be seen and not 'eard, dint you? Everybody dozin' after dinner. You couldn't do owt except creep about. Like clock 'd stopped, 'cept you could 'ear it tickin'.

Cissy It dunt mean what it did no more.

Billy No.

Cissy But summat still creeps up on you round tea time.

Billy Aye. 'Arry Secombe.

Cissy I wonder if they know what's 'appenin?

Alma Who?

Cissy Your dad and all his pals. I wonder if they know what's goin' on today? They must do. Probably there already, standin' in 'shadows, waitin', watchin'.
No, I'd only mek a fool of myself if I went. Don't want to come over queer again.

Alma I told you, it's not eating proper. (*To* **Billy**.) She's had no breakfast.

Cissy I don't need it if I'm not up and about doing.
Sittin' in a bloody chair all day uses up a lot, I'm sure.
Anyroad, you can talk.

Alma I 'ad some toast.

Cissy When?

Alma About four o'clock this morning.

Cissy Were you up then?

Alma Yes.

Cissy I didn't hear you.

Alma You were asleep.

Cissy I've not slept all night. I were countin' bloody
curtain 'ooks at 'alf past three, sat watchin' it get light.

Pause.

Billy Dawn chorus.

Cissy Aye. There's bloody sparrers got in our attic
somewhere. Must be gettin' in some'ow. Frank allus used to
see to that. Bloody 'ouse is goin' to rack and ruin. (*Pause.*)
Let it, eh? It'll outdo me.
We were allus gunna buy a cottage somewhere. I allus
wanted a little stone 'ouse. 'When we come up on 'pools',
he'd say.

Pause.

Billy I got two numbers last night.

Cissy Did you?

Billy I did.

Cissy We never got a thing, did we?

Alma No.

Cissy We do it all on ages, you see, same numbers since
start. But everybody's moved up one now. 'Cept Frank.

Billy What would you do with all that?

Cissy I do it for them. Nice 'oliday for a start.

Billy (*to* **Alma**) You could 'ave a good un for that.

Cissy Couldn't you just. Some new clobber to go in.

Alma It'd be nice.

Cissy I'll win it for you one day. (*Pause.*) Got other one to think about an' all, now.

Alma Would you?

Cissy Course I would.

Alma *smiles at* **Billy**.

(*To* **Billy**.) Do you really think 'e looks like Joe?

Billy Aye. Spit on 'im when 'e were that age.

Cissy (*to* **Alma**) Do you think she'll bring 'im round after?

Alma I don't know.

Cissy Well I shall want to see 'im before they go. I thought I'd give 'im summat of 'is grandad's, only I don't know what. There's nowt 'e'd appreciate.

Billy I told yer yer shouldn't 'a got rid. All that stuff.

Cissy I know, I know.

Billy (*to* **Alma**) I told 'er to wait on. If she'd 'ave 'ad 'er way, I'd a burnt the bloody lot.

Cissy I'm thankful now you didn't listen to me.

Alma So am I.

Billy Aye, your dad's bloody cornet 'd a gone in 'bin if I ant a stopped 'er.

Alma Neville 'ad it out the other week.

Cissy Could 'e play it?

Alma 'E 'ad a go. Anyway, I don't like it fingermarked.

Cissy Your dad could mek it talk, couldn't 'e, eh?

Alma He could.

Cissy Like Angel Gabriel. Remember when I used to tek you both to 'Gala?

Alma I do.

Cissy By, they could play, that band. Made you feel real proud.

Pause.

Billy They'll do 'im proud this morning, Ciss.

Pause.

Cissy He'd fetch it out, latterly, try to blow. He'd just sit and press 'buttons and I 'ad to guess the tune.

Pause. **Neville** *arrives, smart trousers, but still a T-shirt. He carries a plastic 'suit bag' and a shoe box.*

Alma Thanks, Neville. Did you get it all?

Neville I think so.

Alma Good lad. (*She takes the gear.*) What did your dad say?

Neville Nowt.

Alma I'll go and get changed, then. (*To* **Neville**.) You look nice. (*She goes in.*)

Billy Aye, very smart.

Cissy You got a suit on?

Billy 'E dunt need a suit.

Cissy (*to* **Neville**) What you got on, then?

Billy (*to* **Neville**) It's just casual smart, in't it?

Cissy You got a tie on?

Neville No.

Cissy No tie?

Neville No.

Cissy You're not goin' wi' no tie?

Neville Why not?

Cissy Oh, Neville, put a tie on. What you thinking of? Put a tie on for your grandma.

Neville I ant got one.

Cissy There's 'alf a dozen upstairs. Put one o' them on.

Neville I'm all right.

Cissy You're not all right.

Neville I ant got a shirt.

Cissy Oh, he's gunna show me up good and proper.

Billy He isn't.

Cissy What's folk gunna think?

Billy Cissy. He's goin'. That should be enough.

Cissy What about work? Ant you got one for tomorrow?

Neville No.

Cissy What, startin' a new job and no collar and tie? What's your mother thinkin' of?

Neville I don't need one.

Cissy Get yourself upstairs in 'back bedroom wardrobe. Pick a nice white one. There's some lovely ties to go with it an' all. Tootal, not cheap jack. Your grandad picked 'em up at a car boot. Go on, Neville, put one of your grandad's shirt and ties on. Go on, love. Do it for me. He'd be ever so pleased to know you were wearing it. Go on.

Neville *goes in.*

Billy You see? I told you it'd come in, one day.

Cissy   Fancy. What's Alma thinking of?

Pause.

Billy   What IS she thinking of, Cissy?

Cissy   I don't know. Don't ask me.

Billy   She stayed 'ere last night.

Cissy   I don't know what'll come of it.

Pause.

Billy   I just got scared somewhere along my life, Cissy.

Cissy   Give over.

Billy   I don't think like I used to.

Cissy   You think too much.

Billy   Not just scared for me ... for the way things seem to be sometimes, for all of us.

Cissy   Billy, I wouldn't expect owt else off you other than tellin' me the truth. You done that. They needed to know.

Billy   I suppose.

Cissy   I bin prayin' all night.

A car horn pips twice.

Who's this? Is there somebody 'ere?

Billy   I don't know.

Danum *enters. Smart, classy casual.*

Danum   Now then, Billy.

Billy   All right?

Cissy   Danum?

Danum   What you doin'? You goin' like that?

Cissy   Me?

Danum   Come on.

Cissy I'm not goin'.

Danum Why not?

Cissy I never said I was.

Danum You did.

Cissy Did I?

Danum Mam. You did. Weeks ago. I told you I'd come and pick you up.

Cissy You never did.

Danum I did. You said you'd come if I took you.

Neville *comes out. Shirt and tie now.*

Neville Hiya.

Danum Now then.

Cissy (*to* **Neville**) You done it?

Neville Yea.

Cissy Come 'ere. (*He goes to her. She fixes his tie a little.*) That's more like it.

Neville There's a load of games and records in 'bottom of 'wardrobe. Whose are they?

Cissy Most on it's Verna's n' Alma's. Some on it's your Uncle Danum's.

Neville (*to* **Danum**) There's two Monkees LP's. Are they yours?

Danum Verna's.

Neville (*to* **Cissy**) Can I 'ave 'em?

Cissy If she dunt want 'em.

Alma *comes out. Dress, shoes.*

Alma Danum.

Danum Nice.

Alma Thanks.

Billy Aye. Champion. You look lovely.

Danum (*to* **Cissy**) So what's 'appenin' then?

Cissy I can't go, Danum, not in this state. I'd never get in and out of your car, never mind owt else.

Danum Great. (*To* **Alma**.) Do you two want a lift?

Alma No thanks. We'll walk. It's only up the road.

Danum Suit yourself.

Neville You got the Jag?

Danum Yes.

Neville *looks to* **Alma**.

Alma Go on, then. I'll see you there.

Neville Thanks. (*Moves down to* **Danum**.)

Cissy Danum?

Danum What?

Cissy Come round after.

Danum I don't know when –

Cissy I want you 'ere. I want everybody 'ere. Just for a cup o' tea. I've got a tin o' biscuits.

Danum OK.

Danum *and* **Neville** *go. Pause.*

Alma Thanks for his shirt and tie.

Cissy Did he look smart?

Alma Very.

Cissy Better than a bloody T-shirt.

Alma I'll see you later. (*She makes to go.*)

Cissy Alma.

Alma What? (**Alma** *moves back up to* **Cissy**, *kisses her.*)
Bye, Mum. (**Cissy** *takes hold of her arm.*) I know, I know.

Cissy Bye, love.

She lets go of **Alma**. **Alma** *moves off.*

(*To* **Billy**) They don't drink tea, do they, 'young uns. Do
you think I should get some pop? Ought to 'ave an effin
cake.

Billy Eh?

Cissy That were what we allus called 'em.

Billy What?

Cissy Sponge cakes. Special. Allus called 'em effin cakes.
It were our Verna what started it. Her birthday. I came in
one day and I said to her dad 'Oh no, I've forgot the effin
cake'. I never saw her under 'table. She sneaked out and
went to the shop to get it. Next time I went in she says,
'So that's what you call my birthday cakes'. I said, 'What?'
and she says 'Your Verna came in and says "My mam says
can she have her effin cake"'. I din't know where to put
myself.

Pause

Billy Shall I go round shop?

Cissy Aye. Could do.

Pause. Brass band music begins, distant.

Wha's tha want?

Cissy *quiets him with a gesture. They listen. The scene fades.*

Scene Two

Mid-Afternoon

Cissy *in her chair,* **Alma** *and* **Verna** *sat on the edge of the
porch.* **Alma** *is casually looking through a box of old 45s. Next to*

Cissy *is a little fold-up table with a tray of tea things, biscuits.*

Cissy They've not spoke to one another for about, aye, must be twenty year. If he wants owt, he gives her a note. Catholic, you see. He used to be a boxer. I allus thought 'e 'ad funny eyes. He stripped you when he were looking at you. I were allus glad I 'ad on clean underwear. He asked after me, then, did he?

Alma Everybody did.

Cissy I 'ope you told 'em I were incarcerated.

Alma Yes. There were folk even I didn't know, coming up, payin' their respects. (*To* **Verna**.) Weren't there? (*To* **Cissy**.) They all knew who we were, though. Come from all over.

Cissy Who were it'd come up from Skegness?

Alma They told us. I've forgotten. There were that many coming up.

Cissy What did they look like?

Alma He were a smart fella, straight back 'air. Grey. She were dumpy. Glasses. Talked posh.

Cissy No, I can't – It weren't Irene and George Logan were it? I bet it was. They used to 'ave a caravan somewhere down there. I bet it were them. It will a bin. She allus were a bit beyond 'erself. I bet I'm goin' through it now . . . on their way 'ome. 'We come all this way and she can't get off her arse to walk down road'. I'll be 'topic of conversation wi' 'em all.

Alma You won't.

Cissy I should 'ave made the effort.

Alma Everybody understood.

Cissy Did they?

Alma Course they did.

Cissy It sounded lovely. (*Pause.*) And 'vicar 'ad a word did 'e?

Alma Yes.

Alma *pulls out a record, shows it to* **Verna**. *They smile at some memory.*

Cissy 'E's a funny little bloke, in't 'e? I allus thought 'e looked like Miss Piggy. (*Pause.*) I never liked the way 'e shook yer 'and. Clammy. Wouldn't let go, you 'ad to slide your 'and out. He come round about your dad, that day, didn't 'e?

Alma Yes. (*She returns the record, sorts through some more.*)

Cissy Some comfort he was. I don't know who were more embarrassed, him or me. What did 'e say, then?

Alma Just thanked us for coming.

Cissy Aye, well, it were good of 'im I suppose. (*Pause.*) I wish you'd tekken 'camera. (*Pause.*) Never mind.

Alma Somebody'll do you some.

Cissy Aye. Not that I'll be able to see 'em. (*Pause.*) It were a good do, then? Did you cry, pair of you? I'd a bin in a state, no doubt. Once I start I can't stop.

Alma *takes out another record, shows it to* **Verna**. *Again a smile between them at its memory.*

Alma Nineteen seventy . . . four?

Verna Christmas.

Cissy Tek 'em if you want 'em, Verna.

Verna No, it's all right. I 'aven't a record player.

Cissy There's yours in 'loft somewhere. Pity you ant got transport. He could 'ave 'ad that table football game. They 'ad a good go on it, dint they? Him and Neville.

Verna Yes.

Cissy There's still a bag of all your baby gear up there, all of you. I never 'ad the 'eart to chuck it out.

Alma None of mine.

Cissy Yes there is.

Alma I allus 'ad 'ers when she grew out on it.

Cissy I made you some lovely gear, you know I did. There's a bloody bag full of your dolls for a start.

Alma You still got them?

Cissy They're up there somewhere. (*Pause.*) He's a lovely lad, Verna.

Verna Thank you.

Cissy You've brought 'im up good, you can see that. (*Pause.*) Very polite. Shy, just like 'is dad. I tried for long enough to get Joe to call me Cissy. Wouldn't 'ave it, would 'e? Always 'Mrs Cade'. Yet 'e'd call Frank Frank. (*Pause.*) He gets on with Neville all right, doesn't 'e?

Verna Fine.

Cissy I 'ope the bugger dunt get 'em both clartered up wi' muck wherever they've gone, in their Sunday best.

Alma He won't.

Danum *arrives.*

Danum I'm sorry I'm late.

Cissy We'd given you up.

Danum You should 'a bin there.

Cissy Don't tell me. Alma, mek us another pot o' tea, will you?

Danum I'm all right.

Cissy (*to* **Alma**) Go on, love.

Danum Not for me.

Cissy Anybody else?

Verna No thanks.

Alma   No. I'm all right.

Cissy   I'll do wi'out, then. It went off all right, they said.

Alma *gets up.*

Danum   Yes it did.

Alma *moves to* **Cissy**, *takes the tea pot inside.*

Cissy (*to* **Danum**)   That's good.

Danum (*to* **Verna**)   Did you think so?

She nods.

Cissy   Stirred up a lot o' memories for folk.

Danum (*to* **Verna**)   That boy . . . so proud with his mam.

Cissy   She cut 'is 'and.

Danum   Eh?

Cissy   'Eld on to it that tight she cut it with 'er ring finger. Didn't you? He never said a word, did 'e?

Verna   No.

Danum *watches her eyes fill with tears. He is also close to being genuinely overwhelmed by the memory of this morning, but he is still a little scared of her.*

Danum   I'm glad you came.

She looks up at him.

I am. It must a tekken some doin', I know that. You've got some . . . I was real pleased to see you there. I was. (*Pause.*) Bin on me mind all weekend. I . . .

Verna   Have you seen Earl?

Danum   When?

Verna   Since last night.

Danum   No. Well I saw him this morning, like, but not to speak to. He were stood way back. (*Pause.*) Why?

She just looks at him, shakes her head, looks away.

Verna. (*Pause. He sees the box.*) You bin sortin' out your records? Worth a bit, some o' them.

Cissy   Alma 'as.

Danum   Aye.

Cissy   Some on em's yourn.

Danum   We 'ad a good collection between us, didn't we? That *White Album* I 'ad, they're worth a fortune now. And you two nicked it to tek to some party.

Verna   Shirley Tong sat on it.

Danum   Fat arse.

Pause.

Cissy   Weren't that who you got them mucky letters from?

Danum   Get out.

Cissy   I thought so.

Danum   It wasn't.

Cissy   Who were that, then?

Danum   What mucky letters?

Cissy   Your dad laughed and coughed that much he finished up wi' 'is teeth in 'is tea.

Danum   You shunt a bin in me drawers.

Cissy   She were a warm bugger, whoever she was. Weren't her dad a doctor? (*Pause.*) Latest one's a what?

Danum   She left.

Cissy   What does she do?

Danum   Solicitor.

Cissy   Aye, that's it. Solicitor. They're 'andy to know.

Pause.

Danum   She left.

Cissy   I think you must wear 'em out. I never get introduced, needless to say. Bit of a come-down for 'im, bringing 'em round 'ere.

Danum   Mam.

Alma *comes out with the tea pot.*

Cissy   I know, I know. I didn't mean it. (*To* **Alma**.) Thanks, love.

Alma *pours her a tea.*

I can converse proper when I want to, you know. I got a certificate. (*She selects a biscuit from the tin.*) Anybody want a family selection? (*She dunks her biscuit in her tea, eats it.*) These are your dad's favourites. (*She is suddenly tearful, takes out her handkerchief, wipes her eyes.*) I'll never get used to it. I could go mad some days. I could. I could bloody top myself and 'ave done.

Alma   Don't, Mam.

Cissy   I could. (*She cries openly now.*)

Alma   Come on.

Cissy   Nobody knows. Nobody. (*A long pause. She recovers as if nothing had happened.*) Where've they got to? Where's Neville tekken 'im?

Alma   I don't know. Down the river maybe.

Cissy   They've bin a long time.

Alma   I know. Verna's got a bus to catch.

Verna   Don't worry, Mam. It's OK.

Pause.

Cissy (*to* **Danum**)   She cleared off, then, 'solicitor? I thought it were serious? Weren't she movin' in?

Danum She went back to 'er 'usband and three kids.

Cissy She were never married?!

Danum No, she were never married. She got offered a better job away.

Cissy I wouldn't put it past you.

Earl *arrives.*

Danum Now then.

Earl *ignores him, looks at* **Alma**.

What's up?

Earl (*to* **Alma**) Do you want the rest of your stuff fetchin' over?

Pause.

Cissy I've just made a pot of tea if you want one.

Earl (*to* **Alma**) Eh?

Alma *looks to* **Verna**. **Earl** *follows the look.*

(*To* **Verna**.) So you tell me.

Danum Earl, today's not –

Earl Don't. Just don't.

Pause. **Alma** *is tearful.*

Alma You were there this morning.

Earl What?

Alma (*to* **Verna**) And whatever happened this morning, we were all part of it. All of us.

Verna I know.

Alma This village was one again. (*To* **Danum**.) And I can't not think of that. I won't forget it. (*To* **Verna**.) I can't not forget it, Verna. Whatever you think. Whatever else . . .

Cissy Danum?

Danum What?

Cissy Nip in and get me cardy, will you? I'm gettin' a bit chilled. Danum?

Danum *goes in. Pause.*

You're all of you mine. Whatever any of you do in the world, I don't care what it is, I can't stop being your mother. Lord knows I tried wi' you, Verna. Alma'll tell you that. But I couldn't. I can't with any of you. (*To* **Earl**.) Grease monkey included. (*Pause.*) Verna, whatever you do – I'm not telling you what you should or shouldn't do, I'm just … Do you see what I'm saying?

Danum *comes out with the cardigan, puts it over* **Cissy**'s *shoulders.* **Neville** *arrives.*

Alma Where's JJ?

Neville Lookin' at 'car.

Alma Where've you bin? I told you not to go far.

Neville About. Billy Winder's. (*Pause.*)

Danum You all set for tomorrow, then?

Neville Yea.

Alma He's looking forward to it, aren't you?

Neville Yea.

Danum I'll see you're all right.

Verna We'd better mek a move, I suppose.

Cissy What you gunna do about table tennis? Tek it another day?

Danum Table tennis?

Neville Table football.

Danum That's mine.

Cissy You don't want it.

Danum Does JJ want it? Tek it, let 'im 'ave it.

Verna Another day, Danum.

Danum Tek it now.

Verna I can't.

Danum I'll tek you.

Verna No, we're all right.

Danum Let 'im 'ave a ride 'ome. You don't want to be stood waitin' for buses.

Cissy Let 'im go 'ome in 'car. (*To* **Neville**.) Go fetch it for 'im, Neville, will you?

Neville *goes in.*

Verna (*to* **Danum**) Thanks.

Cissy Is 'e comin' in or what?

Verna (*shouting off*) JJ! We're going!

Pause.

Danum I'll get 'im. (*He goes off.*)

Cissy Verna.

Verna *goes up to her, kisses her.* **Cissy** *hugs her. The car starts up, revs.* **Neville** *comes out with the table football game, stands a moment by* **Verna** *who is still being hugged. He looks to* **Alma** *who signals him to take it out to the car. He goes off.* **Cissy** *lets go of* **Verna**. *Both are now tearful.* **Verna** *moves down to* **Alma**. *They hug, move apart.*

Verna JJ! We're going!

The car horn pips twice, the engine revs. **Verna** *looks at* **Earl**.

Bye, Earl.

He manages half a smile. She moves on. Turns.

Bye, Mam.

She goes. Sound of car doors slamming. Two pips on the horn. The car moves off. Pause. **Neville** *comes in.*

Neville   I wanted that.

Cissy   You're too old for that. You're a working man now.

Pause.

Neville   What's 'appenin', then?

Alma   You mean you're 'ungry.

Neville   Yea.

Alma (*to* **Cissy**)   We're going, Mam. (*She moves up to* **Cissy**.)

Earl (*to* **Neville**)   You look smart for a change.

Neville   I feel a prat.

Alma *kisses* **Cissy**.

Alma   See you tomorrow.

Cissy   Aye. I'll be 'ere.

Alma *moves down to* **Earl** *and* **Neville**. *They move off.*

Neville   See you, Gran. Thanks for 'shirt and that. It's really nice.

Cissy   Thank your grandad.

They are gone.

Look after that cornet!

Pause. **Cissy** *closes her eyes. Music – solo cornet practising from inside, as the lights change to night.*

Give it a rest, Frank, will you?! Sounds like an elephant wi' constipation!

The music stops. The lights change back. **Cissy** *is sleeping. Music – a full brass band – fades in, as the lights fade to black out.*

Methuen Contemporary Dramatists
include

Peter Barnes (three volumes)
Sebastian Barry
Edward Bond (six volumes)
Howard Brenton
  (two volumes)
Richard Cameron
Jim Cartwright
Caryl Churchill (two volumes)
Sarah Daniels (two volumes)
David Edgar (three volumes)
Dario Fo (two volumes)
Michael Frayn (two volumes)
Peter Handke
Jonathan Harvey
Declan Hughes
Terry Johnson
Bernard-Marie Koltès
Doug Lucie

David Mamet (three volumes)
Anthony Minghella
  (two volumes)
Tom Murphy (four volumes)
Phyllis Nagy
Philip Osment
Louise Page
Stephen Poliakoff
  (three volumes)
Christina Reid
Philip Ridley
Willy Russell
Ntozake Shange
Sam Shepard (two volumes)
David Storey (three volumes)
Sue Townsend
Michel Vinaver (two volumes)
Michael Wilcox

Methuen World Classics
include

Jean Anouilh (two volumes)
John Arden (two volumes)
Arden & D'Arcy
Brendan Behan
Aphra Behn
Bertolt Brecht (six volumes)
Büchner
Bulgakov
Calderón
Anton Chekhov
Noël Coward (five volumes)
Eduardo De Filippo
Max Frisch
Gorky
Harley Granville Barker
    (two volumes)
Henrik Ibsen (six volumes)
Lorca (three volumes)
Marivaux
Mustapha Matura

David Mercer (two volumes)
Arthur Miller (five volumes)
Molière
Musset
Peter Nichols (two volumes)
Clifford Odets
Joe Orton
A. W. Pinero
Luigi Pirandello
Terence Rattigan
W. Somerset Maugham
    (two volumes)
Wole Soyinka
August Strindberg
    (three volumes)
J. M. Synge
Ramón del Valle-Inclán
Frank Wedekind
Oscar Wilde

Methuen Classical Greek Dramatists

Aeschylus Plays: One
(Persians, Seven Against Thebes, Suppliants,
Prometheus Bound)

Aeschylus Plays: Two
(Oresteia: Agamemnon, Libation-Bearers, Eumenides)

Aristophanes Plays: One
(Acharnians, Knights, Peace, Lysistrata)

Aristophanes Plays: Two
(Wasps, Clouds, Birds, Festival Time, Frogs)

Aristophanes & Menander: New Comedy
(Women in Power, Wealth, The Malcontent,
The Woman from Samos)

Euripides Plays: One
(Medea, The Phoenician Women, Bacchae)

Euripides Plays: Two
(Hecuba, The Women of Troy, Iphigeneia at Aulis,
Cyclops)

Euripides Plays: Three
(Alkestis, Helen, Ion)

Euripides Plays: Four
(Elektra, Orestes, Iphigeneia in Tauris)

Euripides Plays: Five
(Andromache, Herakles' Children, Herakles)

Euripides Plays: Six
(Hippolytos, Suppliants, Rhesos)

Sophocles Plays: One
(Oedipus the King, Oedipus at Colonus, Antigone)

Sophocles Plays: Two
(Ajax, Women of Trachis, Electra, Philoctetes)

Methuen Student Editions

Methuen Modern Plays
include work by

Jean Anouilh
John Arden
Margaretta D'Arcy
Peter Barnes
Sebastian Barry
Brendan Behan
Edward Bond
Bertolt Brecht
Howard Brenton
Simon Burke
Jim Cartwright
Caryl Churchill
Noël Coward
Sarah Daniels
Nick Dear
Shelagh Delaney
David Edgar
Dario Fo
Michael Frayn
John Godber
Paul Godfrey
David Greig
John Guare
Peter Handke
Jonathan Harvey
Iain Heggie
Declan Hughes
Terry Johnson
Sarah Kane
Charlotte Keatley
Barrie Keeffe
Robert Lepage
Stephen Lowe

Doug Lucie
Martin McDonagh
John McGrath
David Mamet
Patrick Marber
Arthur Miller
Mtwa, Ngema & Simon
Tom Murphy
Phyllis Nagy
Peter Nichols
Joseph O'Connor
Joe Orton
Louise Page
Joe Penhall
Luigi Pirandello
Stephen Poliakoff
Franca Rame
Mark Ravenhill
Philip Ridley
Reginald Rose
David Rudkin
Willy Russell
Jean-Paul Sartre
Sam Shepard
Wole Soyinka
C. P. Taylor
Theatre de Complicite
Theatre Workshop
Sue Townsend
Judy Upton
Timberlake Wertenbaker
Victoria Wood